Identity Affir

Learn how to create identity affirming classroom environments that honor the humanity of students.

Although schools have potential to be spaces of inquiry and joy, they can also be the source of trauma and pain when educational equity is not a foundational element. With a race-conscious lens, Dr. Erica Buchanan-Rivera explains how to actively listen to the voices of students and act in response to their needs in order to truly activate equity and make conditions conducive for learning. She also offers insights on how we need to do anti-bias and antiracist work in efforts to create affirming, brave spaces.

Throughout the book, you'll find features such as Mirror Work and Collective Work to help you bring the ideas to your own practice and discuss them with others. You'll also find excerpts from students' voices to hear the why behind affirming spaces through their perspectives. With the powerful ideas in this book, you'll be able to create the kinds of classroom environments that students deserve.

Erica Buchanan-Rivera is an educational equity scholar, consultant, community organizer, and fierce advocate for children and liberatory spaces where people can be their authentic selves. She has served as a teacher, principal, director of curriculum, and adjunct professor. She is currently a Director of Equity and Inclusion in a K-12 public school district in Indianapolis, Indiana.

Identity Affirming Classrooms

Spaces that Center Humanity

Erica Buchanan-Rivera

Routledge
Taylor & Francis Group

NEW YORK AND LONDON

First published 2022
by Routledge
605 Third Avenue, New York, NY 10158

and by Routledge
4 Park Square, Milton Park, Abingdon, Oxon, OX14 4RN

Routledge is an imprint of the Taylor & Francis Group, an informa business

Library of Congress Cataloging-in-Publication Data
A catalog record for this title has been requested

ISBN: 978-1-032-10768-4 (hbk)
ISBN: 978-1-032-04293-0 (pbk)
ISBN: 978-1-003-21696-4 (ebk)

DOI: 10.4324/9781003216964

Typeset in Palatino
by SPi Technologies India Pvt Ltd (Straive)

Access the Support Material: www.routledge.com/9781032042930

To Elise. May all classrooms see you and your brilliance, my child.

Contents

Acknowledgments

Writing a book in a global pandemic while parenting and seeing the world shift from national protests for Black lives to white rage (e.g., insurrection at the US Capitol, educational legislation, and backlash against critical race theory in school board meetings across the country) was an emotional process. I am beyond grateful for the encouragement received from my community, including people who have inspired me to become a better human throughout the journey.

I thank Patricia Payne, a Black nationally recognized educator with 59 years of experience in the field and an antiracist pedagogy expert, who poured into me throughout my student teaching and career as a strong model for justice-centered work. Through her passion, I learned the history I was never taught in K-12 education or a collegiate level, which sparked a desire to pursue more opportunities for growth. She has continuously been a light for me in this work.

There have also been many women of color—Crystal Thorpe, Karen Bush, Renae Azziz, Lanetta Birdsong, Marian Dingle, Dena Simmons, Dennisha Murff, Denita Harris, Jill English, and too many sisters from Alpha Kappa Alpha Sorority, Inc. to name—who have been a healing space for me. I thank them for their encouragement, prayers, and wisdom.

To my legacy, Elise, and husband, Jesus, I love you. Thank you for going through this process with me. I do this work for us and for a world where liberation exists. I could not have finished this book without the support of my husband who shifted his priorities in a heartbeat to provide time for me to write. He has been an amazing partner throughout this endeavor, and I am blessed to do life with him.

Lastly, I thank my parents (Eric and Jackie), sister (Erin), family, friends (especially Casey Schaefer), and co-conspirators from the organization I helped to co-found, the Racial Equity

Community Network (RECN), who have generally been a great support system for me. To my grandmothers who passed before this book was published, I thank you for the wisdom and strength you poured into me. I am also fortunate to have many account-ability partners, including Cornelius Minor, Sara Ahmed, Val Brown, and Rosa Perez-Isiah who offered feedback and wrote reviews for this book. It is a blessing to have so many people affirm and believe in the work I am sharing with the world. I sincerely thank all the contributors of this book and Routledge for the opportunity.

There's power in community and I am overwhelmed with gratitude and love.

About the Author

 **Erica Buchanan-Rivera** is an educational equity scholar, consultant, community organizer, and fierce advocate for children and liberatory spaces where people can be their authentic selves. She has served in education as a teacher, principal, director of curriculum, and adjunct professor in both public and private sectors. During her time as a principal in Lawrence Township Schools in Indiana, she was honored as an Administrator of the Year award recipient and her international school was nationally recognized as a Magnet School of Excellence under her leadership. Dr. Buchanan-Rivera was formerly the Chief Equity and Inclusion Officer in Hamilton Southeastern Schools, the first Diversity, Equity, and Inclusion (DEI) role in a Hamilton county school district in Indiana. She is currently the Director of Equity and Inclusion in a K-12 public school district in Indianapolis, Indiana.

Erica Buchanan-Rivera completed her doctoral degree from Indiana State University in 2017. Her scholarship is centered on identity affirming environments and antiracist pedagogy. She has published many educational articles (including an award-winning ASCD publication in 2019) and her work continues to be in a national spotlight while featured in numerous podcasts, panels, and keynote presentations. Erica Buchanan-Rivera has served as an adjunct professor at the University of Indianapolis and her alma mater, Butler University, where she received the College of Education Distinguished Alumni Award in 2020.

Outside of school systems, she is passionate about mobilizing communities to elevate racial equity. She developed Racial Dialogue Circles (RDCs) within Fishers, Indiana which was designed to ignite conversations about race and justice among people of various racial backgrounds with the intent of participants developing community action plans to address racism. After the implementation of several circles, community members created a coalition called Racial Equity Community Network (RECN), which is a network that provides an entry point for people of all backgrounds to work toward the creation of a just society. Erica Buchanan-Rivera serves as a founding board member of RECN. She also serves on the College of Education Dean's Advisory Board at Butler University. In her personal life, she is happily married to her best friend Jesus and a proud momma. She enjoys cooking, traveling, her church, sharing moments of joy with family, playing her violin, and listening to music as a means to restore her soul.

A Note to the Reader

Identity Affirming Classrooms was born from the narratives of students who mirrored my personal school experiences. Over the span of 30 years, the stories of erasure, invisibility, and institutional racism across contexts remain the same. The pain I harbored from malpractices within educational environments compelled me to join many racial equity-oriented organizations as a youth (often in a leadership role) and study oppressive structures during my collegiate level years. In my graduate program at Butler University for my administrative license, I purposefully choose to study and present on issues pertaining to educational equity. I completed the Pacific Educational Group (PEG) affiliate program during my first year as an assistant principal (2010–2011) and was tasked to conduct district-wide antiracism trainings with Teresa Brown (*Rest in Heaven*) in Lawrence Township Schools in Indiana. Although the learning spaces were challenging, I found it oddly therapeutic to use my voice to speak truth and empower others to actively pursue the work of being an antiracist in the same institutions that often tried to silence me.

My doctoral work focused on inclusive environments and the physical design of classroom spaces. Following the completion of my doctoral degree at Indiana State University, I have been practicing my scholarship in the capacity of DEI roles within K-12, public school districts. I have been invited to speak as a keynote, panelist, and presenter for conferences, webinars, and podcasts across the country. My passion for justice-centered communities has also led to the development of an organization called Racial Equity Community Network (RECN), where people come together to combat racial inequalities.

Through my work, I echo and hold true to the words of US track champion, Sha'Carri Richardson: *I am human.* Speaking publicly and writing a book about affirming spaces does not mean that I am exempt from critique or making mistakes. I am a whole human who recognizes that my knowledge extends as far as the places I have traveled, the people I know, the experiences I have encountered, and the research I have chosen to study. Even with the help of many accountability partners (who graciously read many sections of this book prior to publishing), I know that there are things that will not settle with everyone while existing in a country that has yet to reckon with the systemic nature of racism. Writing a book is a vulnerable process and I hope as I reveal parts of my being, you recognize my human condition as a person who is learning and unlearning every day.

I also started writing this book long before politicians and ideological groups pushed to banned critical race theory (CRT) from schools. In 2020, I was teaching an undergraduate course as an adjunct professor at the University of Indianapolis that focused on educational equity, including CRT, and never imagined that groups across the United States would engage in a concerted effort to stifle DEI work in schools months later. Putting pen to paper amid the wave of backlash against DEI roles (referred to as DIE officers by groups in Hamilton County in Indiana) and antiracist work was hard and cost me many spoons (if you know, you know). These are dangerous, troubling times yet these are also times when truth, honest perspectives, and co-conspirators are needed the most.

My hope is that this book serves as a tool for self-work and helps you to see yourself, to build a critical consciousness, and to be in community with others. I hope it inspires you to become the educator that students need, the teacher that I needed as a child. I hope you continue to be the light during dark times and love children fiercely while recognizing that love isn't enough. And with that understanding, I hope you fight for a world where liberation exists for all and build systems where students know their lives, contributions, and voice matters.

Foreword

The first time I heard Dr. Erica Buchanan-Rivera discuss her work on identity affirming spaces, I felt an urgency for her voice and written word to extend beyond the state conference we were attending. It was the first time we'd met, and I was drawn to her fortitude in the face of a local climate not yet ready for her to disrupt harmful ideologies that immobilize our progress as a nation. With expert cadence and professional generosity, Dr. Buchanan-Rivera brought the room together, allowing participants to process and engage with her life's work—identity development in an intellectually engaging environment.

This book is a gift. The reader is invited into decades of research and experience Dr. Buchanan-Rivera brings to the field, while also being seated front row to the early days of racism and trauma Erica experienced. We do not take her emotional labor for granted. This is never something an author wants to do to make their point, or to bring the reader in. No one should have to revisit pain to bring others along or convince them to believe they need to do better for kids and our nation. However, Dr. Buchanan-Rivera believes in her readers and our ability as educators to get this right for the next generation. The embedded student interviews and anecdotes give voice to this beautifully and authentically as we hear their understanding of belonging and connection to a physical space and a teacher.

Dr. Buchanan-Rivera cites a diverse wealth of scholarship in the global field of education; woven with calls to action, anecdotes, self-reflection exercises, and my personal favorite, questions. With each question, each reflection, the reader is placed into a dialogue with her—Erica becomes your accountability partner in disruption and healing. Dr. Buchanan-Rivera is asking us to normalize conversations of race and whiteness as we commit to intersectional equity work where all means *all*. Erica understands the road to build this capacity for justice is long *and* attainable for us if we commit to naming oppression, disrupting it, and unpacking what has been internalized in us all. This habitual interrogation of the biased systems we have too long stayed wedded to in education will be what moves us forward as a collective.

How fortunate we are to be in partnership with a mentor like Dr. Erica Buchanan-Rivera.

Sara K. Ahmed

Educator and author of *Being the Change: Lessons and Strategies to Teach Social Comprehension*

Introduction

Identity Affirming Spaces

To be seen as fully human is my freedom dream. One's identity is not considered a threat, but rather an integral part in sustaining the power of a community. I ponder spaces where all people can exhale deeply, knowing that their authenticity and intellect are esteemed. You can bring your whole self and neglect cautionary thoughts that constrain capabilities. The energy within the environment yields joy and connection. Your existence matters and the words you speak are acknowledged as a gift. There is atonement and healing in response to harm. We learn how to become better versions of ourselves with each misstep and allow love to lead the way. This is the affirming space I desire for myself, my legacy, and all children who are trying to thrive in an unjust society and inequitable systems within education.

The classroom environment serves as a space for identity development where children learn about their humanity, strengths, and justice. Through social contexts, students also acquire values that adhere to their personhood and adopt ideologies while existing in a sociopolitical, diverse society. As a former early childhood educator, I valued the premise behind Maria Montessori's scholarship. Montessori believed that children absorbed knowledge from their living experiences, including the physical layout and designs of space. She emphasized that an educator's role was to be the custodian of a space that honors authenticity. A rapport should exist between learners and educational spaces that build on cultural strengths.

DOI: 10.4324/9781003216964-1

Bettina Love (2019) lifts the concept of mattering in her book, *We Want to Do More Than Survive*.

> It's an abolitionist practice, rooted in the internal desire we all have for freedom, joy, restorative justice (restoring humanity, not just rules), and to matter to ourselves, our community, our family, and our country with the profound understanding that we must "demand the impossible" by refusing injustice and the disposability of dark children.
>
> (p. 7)

Each educational space conveys a story about safety and belonging. Students learn whether their identity matters through curriculum, the pedagogical approaches or dispositions of educators, policies, peer interactions, and features within a physical environment. The classroom can be a space that nurtures intellectual capacity, promotes joy, and fosters a sense of community. However, the classroom can also reflect oppressive systems and practices that hinder learning experiences and dehumanize the identities of learners. As custodians of space, our beliefs about children and their histories are a critical factor in the creation of an identity affirming environment. The experiences we intend to provide to children are contingent upon the spaces and systems that are created to support instructional practices hinged on our beliefs about equity. The most effective pedagogical approaches can cause harm if implementation derives from a mindset that doesn't see students as fully human.

Pedagogy is defined as the techniques, strategies, and approaches that teachers use within a classroom. As reflective practitioners, we must commit to a process of introspection that empowers us to think about the environment as being synonymous to our beliefs and pedagogy. Lella Gandini (2012) described the classroom environment as "a place where adults have thought about the quality and the instructive power of space" (p. 340). Teachers can reimagine the possibilities and power of space, developing places that honor funds of knowledge and the identities of learners.

As educators, this work starts when we examine how we show up to students. We look deeply at ourselves and deconstruct our identities, reflecting on how we have been shaped to understand lived experiences outside of our own. We intentionally think about our responses, language, and communication with youth and how expressions are internalized or seen in the eyes of children. We process the construction of space and the messages our environments send about mattering. We commit to the dismantlement of structures that harm children and cause them to hide their authentic selves. We are called and have a responsibility to act.

Environment Matters

School environments were the initial places that taught me about the concept mattering, while navigating a system of power that determined who should take up space and who should be forgotten (Love, 2019). As a Black child, I attended a predominantly white, Lutheran school (K-8) in Peoria, Illinois. I functioned in classrooms where no one shared my racial identity or experiences, operating in spaces where only the restroom mirrors validated my presence. My first day of school as a primary student emulated the infamous bus scene from the movie, *Forrest Gump*. After 30 years, I am still haunted by the phrase *"You can't sit here"* that was uttered by white peers during that first bus ride to school. I learned early in my life that my identity and melanin were perceived as problematic. It was my first lesson about mattering while navigating in a space that did not see my Blackness as a strength.

My teachers, mostly white women, had the best intentions at heart, but lacked racial consciousness. They instructed with the colorblind belief that everyone shared the same identity as members of the human race, not engaging in conversations about cultural differences, people of color, or humanity unless centered in a narrative that protected whiteness. Robin DiAngelo (2018) describes whiteness as a socially and politically constructed ideology that yields to an unequal distribution of power based on race. "Whiteness rests upon a foundational premise: the definition of whites as the norm or standard for human, and people of color as a deviation from that norm" (p. 25). It generates a power dynamic that is antithetical to social justice. And in educational systems, whiteness breeds irreparable damage and trauma to students of color who feel their creativity, voice, and identity smothered by a school culture that upholds it.

How do you navigate an environment that embraces the erasure of your identity? What prepares an ethnically, racially, or linguistically diverse student for the shift from affirmations outside of educational spaces (e.g., home, caregivers, family, friends, etc.) to invisibility while operating within school systems? To feel a sense of belonging, there were many times when I had to shed parts of my identity that made me feel whole. I found myself becoming knowledgeable about mainstream culture and literature that did not align with the messaging received from familial structures. Home was fortunately a refuge from the contrasting atmosphere at school. I learned how to navigate two different worlds, switched up my vernacular, and strategically blended in groups to avoid being a focal point. Yet, despite my intentional efforts to assimilate as a child and remain unscathed, I could not escape the fog of microaggressions and racism that I operated within daily.

Psychologist Derald Wing Sue (2010) defines microaggressions as the derogatory slights or gestures that are made toward someone based on their membership of an identity group. In Ibram X. Kendi's (2019) *How to Be an Antiracist*, he refers to microaggressions as racist abuse due to their effects of anger, pain, and distress on people of color. I could not escape the notions that I "spoke well for a Black girl" or that my hair was meant for someone's hand to stroke. As harmful as those experiences were on behalf of peers, it was more damaging to process the responses from adults.

Silence is a response. Inaction is a response. Both of those responses are an adult choice. Most of my teachers did not intervene when racial slurs were projected or when invitations were distributed (from peers) to every backpack but my own, which led to many negative internalizations of my self-worth. When educators who were responsible for my care became aware of my experiences, the responses to hateful rhetoric were anchored in niceness, not justice. *"I'm sure your friend did not mean to call you the N-word. Perhaps, this was all a misunderstanding."* **Misunderstanding**. The only misunderstanding was the inability of educators to disrupt inequitable environments and create spaces that affirmed my racial identity. Whiteness attempted to deplete my magic, but my family and ancestors were the glue that held it together. I chose to attend a public high school that was racially and ethnically diverse. It was a deliberate choice to attend a school with students who shared my reflection. Most of my classes including AP and honors courses had students of color. Although I was initially relieved to interact with faces that shared my resemblance, I learned rather quickly that the presence of Blackness and other racial identity groups did not eradicate whiteness. From curriculum to disciplinary outcomes, whiteness was still at work.

While evolving into my adulthood, I was unsure of the leap I wanted to take professionally. However, I knew my work would center justice, ensuring that children of color felt loved and validated for their experiences. Throughout my years of being a teacher and school administrator, I recognize that many schools and institutions grapple with the confines of whiteness. There is fear when confronting it and resistance from people of all racial backgrounds to change the status quo. When we disregard anti-racist and inclusionary work, we develop spaces where critical consciousness isn't cultivated. There is power in self-introspection and understanding how we've been conditioned to value differences. Neuroscience research conveys that our brain is continuously scanning for threats, and if we don't feel safe, it is difficult to learn or see a world where liberation exists. As educators, we must commit to the work of creating identity affirming spaces and determine how our beliefs either hinder or support the connections we want to establish with students in the classroom environment.

The Common Language of Beliefs, Practices, and Environments

Most of my teaching experiences were spent in early childhood working with kindergarten students. Although I shared earlier my reverence for Montessori's work, I taught in a Reggio-inspired school that focused heavily on the image of children and the development of physical environments that were invitational for learning. Loris Malaguzzi was the founder of the Reggio approach (Edwards, Gandini, & Forman, 1993). Reggio Emilia is a city in northern Italy. The Reggio schools initiated following World War II. Communities needed restoration after the war which prompted the Italian government to provide funding that allowed inhabitants to restore the cultural order with the community. The decision to build a school derived from the belief that the children would advance the future. Malaguzzi, alongside members of the community, built a school via manual labor, brick by brick. He developed the Reggio approach, which "fosters children's intellectual development through a systematic focus on symbolic representation" (Edwards, Gandini, & Forman, 1993, p. 3).

In Reggio, educators view the child as a competent, capable being. Educational practices correlate with a child's identity as a learner (Wurm, 2005). The image of the child is a concept that accentuates the innate strengths of the learners where educators embrace the mindset that the child is powerful; and recognize that learners thrive in physical spaces that optimize learning. Children have the right to learn, imagine, and question their surroundings. Inquiry-based learning sets the tone for the Reggio environment. The educator gives children an opportunity to construct their own knowledge and makes connections to the world around them (Edwards, Gandini, & Forman, 1993).

When thinking about the development of affirming spaces, I cannot emphasize enough the importance of evaluating our beliefs and images of children. We need to interrogate our ideologies and ask ourselves critical questions about the ways our identity influences our interactions with students. I often process how I am showing up to students whose identities are multilayered, including but not limited to racial, cultural, ethnic, linguistic, gender diverse, and religious intersections. The following reflective questions are a part of my ongoing Mirror Work where I self-examine myself:

- What is my image of a learner?
- What do I believe about children including their capabilities and contributions to a learning environment?
- What experiences have shaped my beliefs about children and their identity as learners?
- How do my actions in educational spaces support or negate my constructed beliefs about children?

Beliefs and actions must demonstrate an alignment. If one sees children as intellectual, inquisitive beings, then pedagogical approaches must incorporate provocations, honor imagination, and foster critical thinking. Furthermore, learning should take place in a physical space that is intentionally designed to affirm the image of children and support student-centered, responsive practices. "Strengths are dynamic, contextual, and culturally expressed" (Milner & Ross, 2006, p. 50). Gloria Ladson-Billings (1994) coined the term culturally relevant teaching, which emphasizes the importance of students' learning, the maintenance of cultural integrity, and the development of critical perspectives to confront social inequalities. Geneva Gay's (1999) scholarship has taught us the importance of cultural congruence in teaching and learning practices. Becoming culturally responsive requires us to understand the role of culture and identity within our own lives as well as the experiences of youth, which involves a commitment to mirror work.

What is Mirror Work?

In Sara Ahmed's *Being the Change* (2018), she reminds us that biases are not only something we believe, but a notion that "we act on, operating from many parts of our brain" (p. 45). The biases that we carry into the world, make their way into classroom environments. Mirror work or the examination of self (e.g., identity, biases, ideologies, social awareness, emotional intelligence, etc.), is a critical part of cultural responsivity. It is necessary to know how our beliefs walk in environments and how biases influence interactions with learners.

Mirror work empowers us to reflect on how we value differences, including the messages we have internalized about people outside of our inner circles. We all have biases that program how we respond and engage with others. If you want to understand your social conditioning, you must learn how to unpack yourself. This book will include **mirror work** that serves as a self-check to continuously help you see yourself. You will be offered reflective exercises to process your identity and human development. Give yourself grace through the journey as it will entail learning and unlearning. Here are some initial questions for your consideration.

 **Mirror Work**

Take the time to process the following questions and engage in a journey of self-work.

1. How do I identify? What are the intersections of my identity?
2. Who influenced the way I see myself?
3. When was the first time I learned about differences?
4. How did my family react to people who looked different (i.e., in public spaces)?
5. What messages were conveyed in my household about differences?

While developing or redefining our images, philosophies, and beliefs about students, it's necessary to consider our social construction and how it impacts the learning environment. One may assert that they find value in all students, yet biases can produce actions that communicate otherwise. Mirror work positions us to monitor and check our steps on the venture of pursuing equitable outcomes. This is an ongoing, lifelong process. And it's collective work. Therefore, this book will also incorporate exercises that will require you to process learning with accountability partners, known as **collective work**. When working collectively with others, you'll want to consider norms or agreements for a vulnerable conversation. No one owes you their story, so it's important to remember that point if someone chooses to pass for personal reasons. I do not share everything about my life with everyone, and would not expect others to do the same.

The Classroom is a Life Space

In Kurt Lewin's field theory (1935) the construct of *life space* referred to the locus of an individual's experiences or needs. Lewin (1935) expressed behavior as a function of *life space*. The stimuli within an environment influence how people respond to their surroundings. In my research, I assert that the classroom serves as a *life space* for students who spend most of their time in an instructional setting (Jackson, 1990). Students' perception of the classroom space derives from their identities and lived experiences. Perceptual, diverse individuals will connect to their environments via different entry points. The field theory reminds us of the power of educational environments and the learning spaces we co-construct with students. We thrive in life spaces where beliefs, actions, and environments speak a common language that centers equity and cultural responsivity.

I remember attending a conference that featured a breakout session led by Standing Up for Racial Justice (SURJ). The presenters represented an organization that was designed to call white people into racial equity work and the workshop covered tenets of white supremacy culture. As I listened to the presentation, a fellow colleague signaled for me to look around the room. The workshop was positioned within a high school building in the classroom of a history teacher. While the presenter articulated the tenets of whiteness, I noticed the irony in my colleague's observation that every image on the wall depicted a historical white, male oppressor. I recognized that the facilitators did not have a choice in classroom locations for their presentation, yet I could not help but to wonder about the messages of belonging that were conveyed to adolescents, particularly students of color who functioned within that environment. What does a student internalize when school leaders and teachers convey beliefs of inclusion through vision, mission statements, or core values, but classroom design, content, or approaches reflect stories of dehumanization?

People are not born with a definitive identity (Milner & Ross, 2006). The identity develops due to the *life space* and constructs that individuals adopt (Lewin, 1997; Milner & Ross, 2006). "Architecture and physical design can influence psychological states and social behavior" (Moos, 1979, p. 20). In the context of education, the construct of life space describes the living situations of students that yield to identity development. The classroom, synonymous to one's life space, is an environment where educators can foster identity development and honor the humanity of students. Therefore, pedagogical practices, actions, and physical environments must strategically align to support the genius and cultural gifts possessed by each student.

Identity Affirming Environments

Cultural differences are inevitable in school communities. The contextual experiences of educators may vary from the ways students and their caregivers identify themselves and interface systems. As a part of human nature, we tend to operate through a lens of our living, cultural experiences. Contrary to the weaponization of Maya Angelou's work, *knowing better* does not automatically equate to *doing better*. Awareness is certainly a powerful first step that must be coupled with thoughtful, meaningful, and just actions. Love (2019) conveyed that if we intend to "attack our destructive and punitive educational system, pedagogies that promote social justice must have teeth" (p. 13). This work is about deliberate actions, and it starts with us.

My social conditioning involved seeing the world through a narrow scope, particularly through the schoolings of a Christian-based education which often says... well, we can get into that later. I had to engage in the process of mirror work and learn from many accountability partners to shift my thinking, language, and practices when serving people from different backgrounds. It was a choice I made as a person who is committed to honoring the full humanity of people. I positioned myself in learning experiences to challenge my worldviews, read to feed my soul, and looked for people who loved me fiercely enough to tell me when I needed to collect myself. We will make mistakes and must be willing to repair harm, restore environments, learn from our behaviors, and act with intentionality to do better.

Zaretta Hammond (2015) conveyed in *Culturally Responsive Teaching and the Brain* that educators must develop a sociopolitical consciousness and understand how educational systems yield to unequal outcomes across race and class lines. We need to recognize how our identities determine our navigation and access to systems, understanding the deeply rooted structural barriers that obstruct educational equity. Educators must be cognizant of the ways in which their cultural lens shapes systems or allows embedded inequities to remain unchallenged. We must rededicate our lives to children every day and build authentic relationships, knowing that students only have one school experience (K-12) and the practices of today make a lasting imprint on their future.

Identity affirming schools are grounded in the concept of educational equity, which is the notion of giving individuals what is needed to succeed and thrive. Equity requires an activation of student agency and voice. When unpacking the needs of students through the amplification of their voice, I have found that many racially and ethnically diverse learners mirror my school experience and struggle to feel visible. While working directly with high school students who are a part of gender sexuality alliance (GSA) organizations, I have talked to many adolescents who yearn for gender-inclusive environments, free of practices steeped in heteronormativity. Multilingual learners and students with disabilities have also shared feelings of exclusion due to xenophobia and ableism. Bias, racism, prejudice, and other forms of oppression hinder relationships and foster negative images of self-worth which harms one's identity development. The dismantlement of identity threats involves culturally responsive teaching in an environment that upholds values of affirming spaces and ongoing identity work with students. Importantly, it involves the hard work of identifying and removing structures within systems that make the learning environment emotionally unsafe.

Key Considerations for Affirming Spaces

Identity affirming spaces are safe and brave spaces where students can be their authentic selves. They promote inclusion and acknowledge the intersections of one's identity including sociopolitical contexts. Mirror work is a critical strand in the formation of affirming environments, yet the following demonstrates other important considerations that must be prioritized in the work of establishing classrooms that value one's full humanity.

All Meaning All

The word "all" is a staple, inclusive term used commonly in mission and vision statements, legislations, and policies. However, the term has historically manifested as a catchphrase to disguise the underlying marginalization of underserved groups. *All men are created equal* when colonization, slavery, and exclusionary policies demonstrated otherwise. *All lives matter* when hashtags continue to surface and convey the murders of Black men and women by the hands of white supremacy. *All students can learn* when access, equity, and opportunities lack in educational environments and, as a result, hinder intellectual capacity. *All people are welcomed* when some racial identities feel forced to leave their culture, languages, and authenticity at the door. *All stories have value* when certain narratives are intentionally omitted and erased. Being inclusive is the recognition that all comes with no exceptions. It is a process that involves the methods one uses to deepen interpersonal relationships and co-construct a community.

Decentering Whiteness

It is important to understand the history of white supremacy culture and how it functions in society. Structures that perpetuate whiteness do not have to come in the form of a triangular hood or hate-based organizations. Whiteness can be subtle, operating in policies that disadvantage people of color, practices that lead to a lack of racial representation in specific courses, or instructional content through the projections of falsehoods and stereotypical images. Educators must study whiteness, identify how it infiltrates within schools and themselves, and learn how to decenter it in efforts to build an affirming environment. As Beverly Daniel Tatum (1997) asserted, we have all breathed the smog of racism and whiteness which thrives in institutions. As a Black educator who operated in an environment that erased my racial experience, I must continuously examine how whiteness shows up within my life, thought process, and social interactions.

Being an Upstander

Equity work is a verb that requires action and the role of disrupting the status quo when harmful to children. An upstander uses their voice to speak truth to power and stands up for justice. A culturally responsive educator recognizes that silence in the face of injustice sends a strong message and causes irreparable damage. Silence equals violence. The work of creating identity affirming spaces involves the denouncement of oppressive structures such as racism, classism, ableism, and sexism. We cannot operate with apprehension knowing that lives depend on one's intervention and disruption. Students need to learn about advocacy and allyship. There should also be collective effort among teachers and administrators to support and protect the identities of learners.

Cultural Responsivity

We must be mindful of the histories, culture, and identities of youth. It is necessary to understand the sociopolitical structures that impact the living experiences of students (colleagues too). Culturally responsive practices involve the recognition of students' strengths and the incorporation of approaches that empower learners socially, intellectually, and politically (Ladson-Billings, 1994). It centers the intentional work of cultivating loving, caring communities where students are equipped with tools to advocate for themselves and others. This pedagogical approach, described in Chapter 1, is a commitment to human development and achievement with high expectations held for all children.

The Power of Language

Names and the language tied to our identity hold value and meaning. Words can empower as well as damage others. No one deserves to be exposed to language that devalues their humanity. Culturally responsive educators consider the ways they respond to others and eliminate deficit and coded language (e.g., *those kids, inner city, at-risk, ghetto, drop-outs, etc.*). They reflect on the implications behind language, word choices, and how messages are received, helping students to also understand the abusive nature of microaggressions and eliminate harmful rhetoric.

Components of Affirming Environments

In a quantitative study for my doctoral research, I determined criteria for an identity affirming environment. My research required a factor analysis, which reduces dimensionality through a process that assembles variables into descriptive groupings. In a confirmatory factor analysis, a researcher uses statistical procedure to assess how well measured variables represent the number of theoretical constructs. The methodology is a process that evaluates the measurement model, or the preliminary constructs designed by the researcher. In other words, I developed a series of variables that served as a basis for affirming spaces and tested their validity through an instrumentation process.

Through my research study, five dimensions were developed to help educators think about the components of an identity affirming space. The dimensions included *identity validation, power of community, authentic representation of learning, intentional learning spaces*, and *humanizing approaches*. These dimensions should not be denoted as the only criteria for creating an identity affirming environment. However, this book will highlight the dimensions from my research to spark inquiry and provide practical applications for creating brave spaces that center humanity. The following components are the strands that were verified through research:

Identity validation: features within the classroom environment affirm the identity (e.g., cultural, ethnic, race, class, gender etc.) of learners.

Power of community: classroom environment connects to the natural world, cultural experiences of learners, and inspires authentic relationships.

Intentional spaces for learning: the intellectual capacity of students is honored through the organization of space and instructional materials used for provocations and learning.

Humanizing approaches: the structures and features in a classroom environment that provide learners insight into the educator's equity mindset and enhance learning partnerships with the classroom.

Authentic student expressions: the ways that students represent their individuality, voice, learning, or cultural autobiographies in a classroom environment to build a community that honors the genius and identities of learners.

Each of these concepts will be presented in chapters with reflective questions and practical applications. The components not only connect to the work of educators as custodians of environments but emphasize the importance of partnerships with learners and offer ways to help students be a part of the changes needed to sustain an affirming classroom. It takes collaboration and effort to build a strong community.

Critical Race Theory

The theoretical base for my research that aided in the classification of identity affirming components was critical race theory (CRT). It is a framework that provides an in-depth analysis of race jurisprudence (Delgado & Stefancic, 2001; Milner & Ross, 2006). In the 1970s, a group of interdisciplinary scholars and activists addressed components of the Civil Rights movement that remained undeveloped. The destabilization of racial advancements caused activists to question the practicality in methods used to engender social justice.

Derrick Bell was known as the widely acclaimed frontrunner of CRT. His career pathway intertwined activism, law, and education as a professor at New York University. Bell studied power differentials within race. Theorists, including Kimberlé Crenshaw, Mari Matsuda, and Richard Delgado, were determined to unveil the structures that stewarded discriminatory practices within political systems. Scholars in pursuit of racial equity intentionally examined the intricate dynamics and evolving relationships among race, power, and historical contexts. CRT acknowledges that racism is a normality acutely ingrained in American systems, including education. Therefore, one of the values of identity affirming spaces incorporated the decentering of whiteness within schools.

My work and research elevate the importance of developing race-conscious teachers and educational leaders. You cannot have an identity affirming space in the absence of anti-bias, anti-racist work. Although the creation of affirming spaces is intersectional work, the stories and examples provided in this book will heavily focus on race as a part of my research and identity. In different mediums and publications, you will see me use BIPOC to identify Black, Indigenous, and people of color when discussing racial identities—*and I'm even wary of using that acronym at times due to the complex nature of identities.* However, I will use the terms *people of color* and *white people* in this book to denote power dynamics.

This book is also being written in the middle of a global pandemic, racial unrest, and during a time where a national narrative exists to discredit the scholarship of CRT—*asserting that systemic racism is a fallacy.* People who speak truth to power and denounce white supremacy, including myself, likely encounter backlash, fragility, and malicious attacks. And to be clear, I keep pushing for children ... for my own too. There is a notion that talking about diversity and race is divisive. I challenge that belief and assert that conversations about race are not divisive, but the deficit and racist ideologies people possess that condition their thinking *is divisive.* This book will intertwine various tenets of CRT to maintain the relevance of its value in the creation of affirming environments. However, as a person who has taught CRT on a collegiate level, my acknowledgment of tenets will not capture the depth of the scholarship. As Gloria Ladson-Billings (2013) conveyed in *The Handbook of the Critical Race Theory in Education*, we cannot understand the core concepts of CRT and its relation to the field of education without an analysis of the legal literature the theory derived from. I want to emphasize that this book will provide context for the implications of CRT in education but will not fill all voids of knowledge surrounding the theory. Yet, I would encourage you to read work from critical race theorists and the originators to learn more, not from the uninformed right-wing bases who are deeming any word tied to liberation as CRT.

About this Book

The first section of the book will focus on the internal work and understanding adults need to possess before implementing strategies with an attempt to create an affirming space. Any strategy placed in the hands of someone who has not engaged in critical reflections and self-examinations could be used as a weapon against children at the margins. The work of creating equitable environments and affirming spaces is not a quick-fix solution. You cannot apply a bandage to a systemic issue and expect its complexities to magically disappear. This work is hard, challenging, and will require you to come back to the drawing board often with frustration, yet it is worthy labor that makes a difference in the lives of children. We must be committed to work through the process. Mirror work will be emphasized heavily throughout this book. I believe that we can be our biggest barrier in this work due to our social conditioning and the misconceptions many of us have internalized about identity, power, and race throughout our existence. The first section will unpack the following concepts:

- ◆ the political nature of educational environments;
- ◆ anti-bias, antiracist work, and forms of oppression;
- ◆ the historical and sociopolitical contexts of American schools;

- whiteness in education;
- culturally responsive pedagogy;
- educational equity;
- race-conscious educators.

The second section of this book will focus on the dimensions from my research. Each chapter will feature components that will help to paint the picture of an identity affirming environment. Educators will think about the validation of one's identity, spaces of belonging and collaboration, and the ways students express their learning. There will be practical applications provided and reflective questions to challenge thinking. I want to emphasize that my research is not prescriptive nor the anecdote to an inequitable environment. It is a framework to guide educational equity that relies heavily on the disposition and beliefs of educators. I cannot convince anyone to love all children—it's not my work. However, I can help you to think about the formation of your beliefs and leave the rest to you.

References

Ahmed, S. (2018). *Being the Change: Lessons and Strategies to Teach Social Comprehension*. Heinemann.

Delgado, Richard, & Stefancic, Jean. (2001). *The Critical Race Theory: An Introduction*. New York, NY: New York University Press.

DiAngelo, R. (2018). *White Fragility: Why It's So Hard for White People to Talk About Racism*. Boston, MA: Beacon Press.

Edwards, C., Gandini, L., & Forman, G. (Eds.). (1993). *The Hundred Languages of Children: The Reggio Emilia Approach to Early Childhood Education*. Norwood, NY: Ablex Publishing Co.

Gandini, L. (2012). The observant teacher: Observation as a reciprocal tool of professional development: An interview w/Amelia Gambetti. In C. Edwards, L. Gandini, & G. Forman (Eds), *The Hundred Languages of Children: The Reggio Emilia Experience in Transformation* (3rd ed.). Santa Barbara, CA: Praeger.

Gay, Geneva. (1999). *Culturally Responsive Teaching: Theory, Research, and Practice*. New York, NY: Teachers College Press.

Hammond, Z. (2015). *Culturally Responsive Teaching and the Brain.* Thousand Oaks, CA: Corwin.

Jackson, Philip W. (1990). *Life in Classrooms.* New York, NY: Teachers College Press.

Kendi, I. (2019). *How to be an Antiracist.* New York, NY: Penguin Random House.

Ladson-Billings, Gloria. (1994). *The Dream Keepers: Successful Teachers of African American Children.* San Francisco, CA: John Wiley & Sons.

Ladson-Billings, Gloria. (2013). Critical race theory—what it is not! In Marvin Lynn & Adrienne D. Dixson (Eds.), *Handbook of Critical Race Theory in Education.* Routledge.

Lewin, K. (1935). *A Dynamic Theory of Personality.* New York, NY: McGraw.

Lewin, K. (1997). *Resolving Social Conflicts: Field Theory in Social Science.* Washington, DC: American Psychological Association.

Love, B. (2019). *We want to do More Than Survive.* Boston, MA: Beacon Press.

Milner, E., & Ross, W. (Eds.). (2006). *Race, Ethnicity, and Education* (4th ed.). Santa Barbara, CA: Praeger.

Montessori, Maria. (1964). *The Montessori Method.* New York, NY: Schocken Books.

Montessori, Maria. (1965). *Dr. Montessori's Own Handbook.* New York, NY: Schocken Books.

Moos, Rudolf. (1979). *Evaluating Educational Environments.* San Francisco, CA: Jossey-Bass.

Sue, Derald Wing. (2010, November 17). *Microaggressions: More than Just Race.* Psychology Today.

Tatum, Beverly. (1997). *"Why are All the Black Kids Sitting Together in the Cafeteria?" and Other Conversations About Race.* New York, NY: Basic Books.

Wurm, J.P. (2005). *Working in the Reggio Way: A Beginner's Guide for American Teachers.* St. Paul, MN: Redleaf Press.

Part I

Do the Work

As a consultant and professional in a DEI role, I am often asked by others, *"Where do I begin?"* as related to justice-centered work. My answer is that people should begin with a deep analysis of themselves. If we want to fight for others, we must know *how we show up* into the work of creating equitable outcomes. In my career, I have witnessed people show up with their heart in the right place, but their minds did not reflect a critical consciousness to authentically love children who did not share their identity or lived experiences. I was also an educator who came into the field with the best intentions but recognized quickly that I had so much to learn and that my lack of knowledge contributed to actions that negated my beliefs about children. When I rededicated my life to a process of learning and unlearning, I could feel a shift in my pedagogy, leadership, and my humanity. I have made plenty of mistakes and still fall short at times, but I am committed to looking in the mirror and connecting with people who can hold me accountable. This section will walk you through the internal work that is needed prior and during the work of developing identity affirming environments. We all need an understanding of historical contexts that have shaped our current realities and a common language of educational equity that is rooted in justice and love for the children as well as communities we serve.

DOI: 10.4324/9781003216964-2

1

The Role of the Classroom and the Sociopolitical Contexts of Schooling

Reduction of injustice is not the same as freedom.
Ella Baker (as cited in Jones & Hagopian, 2020, p. 132)

The classroom environment, encompassing the disposition and beliefs of educators, pedagogical approaches, and socialization, is one of the most influential factors in identity development. Carla Shalaby (2017), educator and author of *Troublemakers*, conveys that classrooms are places where we must practice freedom. Liberatory spaces are not created by chance, but through intentional and equitable actions rooted in justice, collectivism, and accountability. The classroom should provide opportunities for dreaming, fostering a love for self and imaginative thinking that isn't distorted by systems of surveillance. Students should be able to take risks in an inclusive, democratic culture that centers joy.

As an administrator, I have witnessed the good intentions of educators transcend into harmful actions. I have engaged in critical conversations with adults who were unaware of their own role in fracturing student relationships. Through policy work,

DOI: 10.4324/9781003216964-3

I have seen leaders come to the table and debate the humanity of students, including my own. At educational conferences, I have sat through trauma-informed sessions that rarely discussed the trauma that happens *within* the walls of a classroom environment. My work has been devoted to helping people see what they don't acknowledge and how they show up in the eyes of children.

Our ability to see each other as fully human involves ongoing mirror work and understanding the sociopolitical contexts within society. Nieto and Bode (2017) define sociopolitical contexts as the laws, policies, ideologies, and practices that generate unequal outcomes and the marginalization of identity groups. The political, social, and economic structures within society influence and frame the decisions made within education. People in positions of power determine what constitutes a developmentally appropriate curriculum, who should receive an invitation into academic or social programs, what narratives in history should be acknowledged, and what should be recognized or celebrated. While writing this book in a global pandemic, it's also not lost on me that directives pertaining to the reopening of schools were overtly political. The field of education is inherently political, and the decisions made by humans within systems shape the experiences of those who are a part of the institution.

As a student, I was not exposed to a curriculum that incorporated authors of color. I internalized ideologies of whiteness and believed I had to prove my worth since I could not see my racial identity reflected. The students I have served over the span of my career have also shared disheartening narratives about the ways school environments steal joy, creativity, and deflate the pride one has for one's culture. Muslim school-based student organizations have conveyed that outside of their safe space, their culture is only acknowledged within courses in the context of terrorism. Within an intersectional club that I co-sponsored called Student Alliance for Equity (SAFE), high school students would share that they did not want their mental health, race, or ability to define how others treated or perceived them and recognized how school structures magnified disparities. Students are constantly processing the messages school environments send about mattering.

Erasure thrives in oppressive environments where political decisions deny basic human rights and the ability to bring one's whole self into educational experiences. Students know if their identities are reduced to a test score or the categorization of a high, low, or average ability group. They are also acutely aware of the identities that not only have a seat at the table but have the universal key to access every opportunity. I have worked with elementary students who can articulate how biases of adults come to life. Children recognize who and what matters in school settings, providing me some of the most insightful lessons I have learned as an educator. Shalaby (2017) asserted that "we need schools that offer young people a chance to grapple with these lessons—schools fueled by the imperative to imagine and to create a world in which there are no throwaway lives" (p. xviii).

The classroom is a space where learners can process the structural and educational inequities that exist and co-construct welcoming environments with teachers. However, it is critical for all educators to understand the depth of institutionalized racism, stereotype threats, and their role in dismantling injustice. Civil rights activist, Ella Baker, said that "reduction of injustice is not the same as freedom." We must understand how forms of oppression operate, dissemble foundations that uphold inequities, and rebuild systems to support as well as affirm all identities.

Antiracism and Education

An identity affirming environment prioritizes anti-bias and antiracist work (ABAR). We all have biases that derive from our experiences and form the ideologies we carry into the world. Elena Aguilar (2020), in *Coaching for Equity*, equates racism to a toxic substance that is not only in the air we breathe, but in the soil in which we plant crops and the water we drink. In other words, racist ideologies permeate our physical, emotional, and social beings and we—*white people and people of color*—must learn how to confront white supremacy culture. Furthermore, we have to move beyond identifying the manifestation of whiteness in institutions and learn how to dismantle the racism that is deeply ingrained in curriculum, policies, and school culture.

Racism is prejudice plus power, a system of oppression that rests on the belief that one race is superior to another based on physical characteristics. It robs one's humanity and dreams of freedom. Those who engage in antiracism surrender themselves to the work of disrupting racism every day. It's about centering and listening to people of color, understanding needs, and shifting the power dynamics to create and sustain access, opportunities, and resources for identity groups that have historically experienced marginalization. Antiracist work has always existed as a response to racism. Many people throughout history, including Sojourner Truth, Fred Hampton, Grace Lee Boggs, Claudette Colvin, and John Lewis, fought for liberation and organizers across the country continue to mobilize others to fight against racism today. Antiracist work requires ongoing mirror work— *you'll hear that again and again*—where we challenge the pollutants that have clouded the ways we see other racial identity groups or ourselves.

ABAR, which is prevalent in many Montessori schools, is an approach that works to eradicate discriminatory practices within education. Biases can lead to damaging patterns. We must recognize how our biases influence our communication, interactions, and the ways we empathize with people. Furthermore, we must learn how to equip ourselves with tools to talk about racism, whiteness, and white supremacy culture. Conversations about race and the disruption of racism should be normalized.

Identifying Oppression within School Environments

My sixth-grade experience is etched in my memory as the year I amplified my voice and, as Congresswoman Maxine Waters would say, "reclaimed my time." It was the year I decided to no longer internalize the pain of erasure in silence and vowed to tell someone when my identity felt threatened. Unfortunately, that someone was a teacher who I trusted; a relationship that was tainted due to the releasing of harbored racist ideologies. I was reading independently and sitting in the front of the classroom. The room was quiet except for a few white males who were talking in the background. And, important to note, I was the only Black student within the classroom. The teacher warned the boys to watch their voice levels a few times and to stop making beats in the back of the classroom. Finally, she reached a point of frustration and I assumed she was going to separate the group or call for the support of a neighboring colleague who typically escorted peers into his room for a "break." However, this time she yelled without hesitation, *"You guys need to stop acting Black!"*

The broken record sound that you hear in any motion picture during a climactic event cued in my brain. Almost immediately, I dropped my book and looked around the class to survey reactions. I will never forget how I felt as my eyes danced around the room and I recognized that no one had flinched. My body froze. I questioned my existence. *How did she see me … my racial identity as a student? Did she see my Blackness as a deficit?* Following class, I approached my teacher and shared how her words made me feel. She was embarrassed and led with defensiveness, feeling inclined to share that she did not consider herself a racist. The next day she gave me a lengthy apology note that expressed how her biases and stereotypical views were hurtful. She deconstructed herself before my eyes, showing me how racism affects all of us. And, I still have this note today, one artifact of many to symbolize the racial trauma I experienced in classrooms.

The oppressive structures (e.g., *racism, classism, sexism, etc.*) that exist in school settings are impediments to the creation of an affirming space. Therefore, it is important to name the barriers that hinder the outcomes and success of students and eradicate the inequities that challenge the liberatory environments we are striving to create for students. Jamila Lyiscott (2019) developed the Fugitive Action Framework referenced in her book, *Black Appetite, White Food*, to confront the role and presence of whiteness on a micro and macro level within society. The framework acknowledges four forms of oppression that show up in education and across other industries.

Ideological: collective consciousness, beliefs and ideas upheld about various groups.

Institutional: the network of institutional structures, policies that create advantages and benefits for some, and discrimination, oppression, and disadvantages for others.

Interpersonal: the ways that ideological, institutional, and internalized privilege and oppression play out in everyday interactions between members of privileged and oppressed groups.

Internalized: the process in which a member of an oppressed group accepts the stereotypes applied to the group by its oppressors.

When reflecting on my sixth-grade experience, I recognize that the four forms of oppression were at work. There was a shared belief about the behaviors of Black people as confirmed by the teacher's statement and the indifference of white peers. The anti-Black messages in society conditioned a collective consciousness among fellow classmates who did not decipher the harm from the statement. Since the narratives of people of color were not prioritized or acknowledged, the institution conveyed a message about mattering whether explicitly stated or not. Although we prayed for all lives in chapel, it was clear that the gifts, strengths, and stories of Black people were discounted.

I had to navigate interpersonal oppression with an adult as a child and put myself in a position to do the heavy lifting to tell someone how they made me feel unsafe. Despite speaking out and elevating my voice, I still internalized a message of anti-Blackness that day and strived to operate in ways that would not allow me to be seen as a disruption. This is one example of how whiteness can function in people of color. When I say we have work to do, I am including all shades of color in this work.

 **Mirror Work**

This is the time to get personal and real with yourself. Grab a journal or notebook and a writing utensil to map out your thoughts. There is growth on the other side of the mirror if we take time to study our own image and how it was constructed. Please process and answer the following:

◆ When did you learn you possessed a racial identity?
◆ What racial identities did you affiliate with as a child?
◆ How did your social contexts influence your attitude and beliefs surrounding racial diversity?
◆ How have you been exposed to racism and what societal message did that experience communicate to you?
◆ What does it mean to you to be an antiracist?

To white educators starting an antiracist journey, you may feel uncomfortable when thinking about race or talking about racism. It may be challenging to confront a system of power that you have benefited from. However, in a field that demonstrates whiteness as property (Harris, 1993) due to the majority of faculty and administrators being white—*a CRT tenet that speaks to the dominance of power and protection of status (e.g., access to positions, tenure, etc.)*—it is imperative to identify how white supremacy culture is evident in schools. Being an antiracist involves ongoing mirror work. It's acknowledging the truth about the origins of racism. Laura Rinderknecht (personal email, 2021), co-conspirator and core trainer for Standing Up for Racial Justice in Indianapolis, IN (an organization that calls white people into antiracist work) has shared that the work is not about shame and guilt:

> It is about taking responsibility for your thoughts, actions, and biases. We are all socialized in a culture that devalues certain populations; that is in all of us. It's not about feeling shame or guilt, but it IS about taking responsibility for ourselves – our thoughts, our biases, and our actions. Left unexamined, we [white people] can unintentionally harm the students that we serve. We must do our own deep and sometimes uncomfortable internal work. We have to analyze the messages that we've received and do a whole lot of unlearning.

Understanding racism requires self-work that no one, particularly people of color, can do for you. As this book progresses, continue to lean into discomfort and embrace the mirror as well as collective work. Rinderknecht (personal email, 2021) often states, "there is no end point in this work and white people shouldn't go into it expecting a cookie or trophy. There is always more room to grow and learn."

To educators of color, it may be difficult to think about the trauma from racism. I do not want you to feel as if you have to relive those experiences. However, I do think it is important for us to recognize how we have absorbed societal messages about our existence into our schema and how they frame the work we do with students. I also recognize that identities are complex and racial experiences are not monolithic as each person's social construction is different. There have been plenty of conversations in my lifetime with people who look like me, who view principles of equity as means to victimize communities of color and refrain from liberatory work—*and truthfully, those have been some of the hardest discussions I have navigated*. Without an ongoing self-assessment, anyone, whether cognizant of forms of oppression or not, can unknowingly uphold whiteness. As educators of color, we also must prioritize our well-being while functioning in spaces that are on a journey but need decades-worth of work before becoming an equitable environment. Some of us fight the good fight at the cost of our own mental and physical health and need to commit to radical self-love.

Examining Classroom Design, Historical Contexts, and Whiteness in Education

Antiracist work requires us to be race-conscious educators (Buchanan-Rivera, 2019) who intentionally work to decenter whiteness in education and eliminate barriers that marginalize students of color. We must be mindful of how curriculum, school policies, and adopted practices are partial to whiteness and the ways many of us—*including people of color*—have been accustomed to doing school in a field led by predominantly white educators in state and local levels. At the heartbeat of racism is white supremacy. Therefore, we must identify how white supremacy culture is evident within our schools, recognizing the origins of racism and actively working to eradicate it. This book will not reveal all the pertinent histories relevant to whiteness in education yet will highlight the beginnings of classroom design to emphasize how white supremacy culture, manifests in schools. Knowing history helps us to become cognizant of the permanence of racism and how it has been universally embedded in systems legally, which is a power analysis that CRT explores (Delgado & Stefancic, 2001). Literature such as Roxanne Dunbar-Ortiz's (2015) *An Indigenous Peoples' History of the United States*, Isabel Wilkerson's *Caste* (2020), and Jeanne Theoharis' (2018) *A More Beautiful and Terrible History* also enhance understandings that reveal the shaping of inequities that plague humanity.

Emergence of Whiteness in American Schools

The dehumanizing method of domineering one's land and creating structures to uphold new systems, laws, religious beliefs, and government is historically known as colonization (Singh, 2019). American history is saturated with stories of dehumanization via the colonization of Indigenous peoples and the enslavement of Africans to justify structures of capitalism. For Indigenous peoples, relation to land is central to identity, culture, and existence. The connection is reciprocal where land sustains and provides a source of strength for humanity, while people serve as stewards who care for natural resources (Dunbar-Ortiz, 2015). Indigenous people and land are a cohesive, ecological organism (Cajete, 2015) that honors a governance anchored in collectivism, a practice of valuing the needs of a community over individualism.

Contrary to stereotypical images of Indigenous living in historical texts, there were cities, towns, roads, and many other developments that whiteness has strived to erase from history (Dunbar-Ortiz, 2015). Colonialists had no relations to land and were deeply invested in methods of subjugation and exploitation. Robin Wall Kimmerer (2013), scientist and member of the Potawatomi Nation, conveyed in *Braiding Sweetgrass: Indigenous Wisdom, Scientific Knowledge, and the Teachings of Plants* the following:

In the settler mind, land was property, real estate, capital, or natural resources. But to our people, it was everything: identity, the connection to our ancestors, the home of our nonhuman kin-folk, our pharmacy, our library, the source of all that sustained us. Our lands were where our responsibility to the world was enacted, sacred ground. It belonged to itself; it was a gift, not a commodity, so it could never be bought or sold.

(p. 17)

Colonialists used religion as a shield to justify dehumanization. Historically, there have been accounts of people using religion as a weapon or tool of whiteness against marginalized communities to inflict harm through acts of violence, unjust laws (*such as the rhetoric surrounding multiple anti-trans legislations in several states*), or as noted in my school experience, to erase racial identities through colorblind approaches (i.e., *"We're all humans,"which has been translated in modern times to "All Lives Matter"*). Stories of resistance are entrenched in lands of the United States, which are narratives that have been omitted by design within education. The blueprints and standardization of American schools were built on stolen Indigenous territories and dreams of white supremacy. Let's start with the colonial period and talk about the physical structure and designs of American schools.

In 1642, the Massachusetts Bay colonists initiated the first enactment of laws pertaining to literacy which penetrated teachings of colonial culture within education. The law of 1647, also known as the Old Deluder Satan Act, mandated a structural space in promotion of educational practices where children could learn how to read and interpret the bible (Urban & Wagoner, 2014). This law required colonies to educate children and was known as the basis of public education in American schools. The emergence of laws prioritized the development of buildings for instruction which marked the start of many educational configurations rooted in whiteness. School facilities populated throughout the mid and late 1600s. The pendulum of education shifted from an emphasis on cultural and religious beliefs to academic content areas of focus including classical literacy. Colonial leaders constructed utilitarian spaces for instruction.

Common School Movement

One-room schoolhouses became a common, multi-purpose site for learning during the colonial era throughout the age of the Enlightenment. Schoolhouses served as community centers, places for worship, and destinations for forums. Advancing to the Jacksonian era of the mid 1800s, President Andrew Jackson's political influence ignited the rise of the Common Man movement, which referred to the recognition of underrepresented classes not inclusive of people of color. The Whig political party generated platforms for education during the Common Man movement (Urban & Wagoner, 2014). Horace Mann and Henry Barnard promoted the idea of the *common school*, which emphasized the development of non-sectarian, public institutions with uniformity in curriculum (Kirst & Wirt, 2009). Curricular subjects under the common school movement were diversified to include music and art, physical education, science, and language development.

Horace Mann was the secretary of the Massachusetts Board of Education. The implementation of pedagogy became a focal point of interest for Mann who revered the concept of object teaching (i.e., learning starts with observations of objects to enhance students' understanding of concepts) based on the work of theorist Johhann Heinrich Pestalozzi. Horace Mann led reforms that challenged educational leaders to reflect on the layout of space in classrooms. Mann's standard design for schoolhouses included rows of desks that faced the direction of an instructor—*teacher-directed instruction*. The proposal of school design under Mann's leadership also required the blackboard positioned in the front of the classroom with windows on two sides of the room. Educators raised their desks on platforms, which allowed them to maintain visibility throughout the room. The spatial organization of the room distinguished the role of the educator as an authoritative figure. We still see this design and organization of classroom spaces in some schools today (Figure 1.1).

W	Chalkboard	W

Teacher desk

Pupil				
Pupil				
Pupil				

FIGURE 1.1 Horace Mann's Classroom Layout (adapted from Weisser, 2006)

Mann and Barnard proclaimed that the spatial organization of a classroom should intrinsically narrate the purpose of educational programs. Barnard's reforms throughout the Northeast in the mid 1800s also revealed the importance of the architectural shell of a school building (Weisser, 2006). As the populations grew within cities and towns, social reformers focused their efforts on infrastructural developments and school buildings.

Standardization of School Designs

The Industrial Revolution progressed amid school design reforms of the 1800s. Child labor laws mandated school attendance, which led to overcrowded educational institutions. The standardization of school designs became a necessity due to the upsurge in student enrollment (Pai, Adler, & Shadiow, 2006). The former wave of one-room schoolhouses evolved into larger facilities with purposeful spaces including cafeterias, laboratories, gymnasiums, and auditoriums. Reforms in New York City and various metropolitan areas focused on the modernization of outdated facilities.

As developments and educational reforms were becoming vastly pervasive, communities of color continued to resist and revitalize, despite oppressive systems and histories of colonization and the diaspora.

Kimmerer's (2013) story of Indigenous wisdom conveyed that power has two sides: *the power to destroy and the power to create.* White supremacy was an arrangement of power used to protect whiteness via destructive actions and government sanctioned laws against racialized groups, and through resistance, historically marginalized communities invested their power in creation and liberation. For example, Black literary societies were developed in the early 1800s in northern cities such as New York, Boston, and Philadelphia (McHenry, 2002; Muhammad, 2020). In these regions, Black people free from enslavement created communities that centered literature, language, mathematics, science, and English. Despite racial inequities and the sociopolitical climate, Black communities devised forums and spaces of self-empowerment as well as collective learning, meeting in churches, classrooms, and private homes.

> There's strength in resistance, and through resistance, power is reclaimed.

As more school facilities were developed in the 1900s, published works emerged regarding the standards, evaluations, and construction of school buildings (Hamlin, 1910). Publications not only described the layout of space but also focused heavily on the ventilation (to mitigate the spread of tuberculosis) and lighting of classrooms. Architects emphasized the importance of outdoor air and natural lighting within building design plans. Classroom design standards called for light to project over the left shoulder of children within the environment to acknowledge the dexterity of right-handed individuals. By the time of the Great Depression in the 1930s, architects established guidelines for lighting, safety (i.e., inclement weather, square footage per student, etc.), ventilation, and sanitation for school design reforms. The Public Works Administration (PWA) utilized funding to build schools in response to the Great Depression (Weisser, 2006).

Intentional Pause for Reflection

Let's pause for a moment, catch our breath, and take some time to debrief. Schools in the United States were developed on Indigenous lands, seized by force. Structural and institutional forms of oppression stripped away human rights from communities that were not a part of the arrangement of white supremacy.

Schools were developed for cultural preservation to maintain the doctrines of religious beliefs that also justified exclusion, dehumanization, and assimilationist ideologies. The intricate, architectural designs of school environments from *the dimensions of space to the organization of furnishings, placement of lighting, and student-centered features* were developed to support pedagogical approaches that benefited the "whole-child"—*able-bodied, white children*. In the most literal sense, American schools were not built for the existence and cultural identities of children of color. Yet, the fight for freedom, ancestral lands (e.g., Onondaga Nation, Dakota Access Pipeline, etc.), and an equitable society has never ceased. The power to create in an unjust world has never ceased. We all hold that power.

The Aftermath of *Brown vs. Board* (1954)

The *Brown vs. Board of Education* (1954) decision ruled that racial segregation within public education was unconstitutional. Although this ruling was known as one of the most pivotal milestones for civil rights, there were many unintended consequences for communities of color. The onset of American educational spaces, architectural designs, and curriculum centered whiteness. Children of color were not integrating into spaces that recognized their brilliance or affirmed their racial identities. Following the decision, nearly 38,000 Black educators were either demoted or forced to resign as white superintendents began to integrate schools (Lutz, 2017; Murff, 2020). The student population increased by nearly two million pupils between 1958 and 1968 (Hille, 2011).

The 1964 Civil Rights Act barred segregation and discrimination based on race, gender, religion, or national origin (Horton & Horton, 2001). Bilingual education also became an integral part of schools in the 1960s in response to the influx of multilingual learners immersed in an all-English curriculum (Urban & Wagoner, 2014). Congress passed the Bilingual Education Act in 1968, which opened the doors to multilingual instruction and practices for language acquisition. The 1970s marked the start of multicultural education, which led to culturally responsive pedagogy.

Among other unintended consequences, as outlined in Martha Minow's (2010) *In Brown's Wake*, the following material-ized after the *Brown vs. Board* ruling:

1. Advocacy for gender equality in public education.
2. Inclusion for students with disabilities.
3. School choice.
4. Approval to use public funds in support of religious, pri-vate education.

The aftermath of *Brown vs. Board* reveals many social movements across race, class, ability, gender, and language. Unfortunately, the backward design of desegregating schools in absence of conscious integration efforts and culturally responsive teaching demonstrates many costs today. School leaders are still grappling with how to decenter whiteness in educational environments.

Whiteness shows up in curriculum when history and litera-ture is presented from a Eurocentric worldview. It permeates in policies that dictate hairstyles and dress codes, which disregard the cultural, ethnic, and religious identities of students (e.g., *stu-dents of color receiving detentions or punitive consequences over hairstyle policy violations*). There are traces of whiteness in standardized testing and program criteria that yield to a lack of racial rep-resentation in specialized courses (e.g., *AP, Honors, enrichment programs, etc.*) in schools. It moves in professional development experiences that consist of all white panelists or white speak-ers who talk about "best practices" in education while people of color are assigned to talk about race. The languages and vernacu-lar that are deemed as acceptable within a school culture speaks to whiteness in motion. Establishing Juneteenth as a federal holi-day amid the tampering with Black voting rights and the push to ban conversations about race in schools speaks to the ways whiteness operates.

Within my work in schools and as a community organizer, I talk about healing spaces for students of color who feel the weight of oppressive systems. Oppression harms everyone and causes dysfunction within society (Cajete, 2015). It cannot be dismantled unless it's named and interrogated, accompanied by a disruption process that will be described in Chapter 2. The following are thoughts from two former, Black male high school students who were willing to unpack their navigation in systems of whiteness to provide context of what is internalized in school spaces:

> Whiteness in education is everywhere. From the kids in the halls to the curriculum that is taught. Being at a predominantly white school makes you feel like you're held to a higher standard. They [teachers] want you to be perfect. In a sense, you could say they want you to be "white." They are harder on Black kids for doing the same things as a white kid. They teach certain parts of the history book and skim over my history. They want to seem like the heroes instead of revealing the full truth. When we do go over African American History, it is only for one day. Teachers go over the same people every year such as Dr. MLK Jr., Rosa Parks, and Malcolm X. After that it's back to "white" history. In the hallways, teachers favor certain students. They can call their names from one side of the hallway to another, but when an African American student walks by, it's almost like they are not there. When it's time to pick committees and leaders, there are the same 3–4 token Black people chosen. After that, it is all white and nobody else is chosen. The whiteness in education is all around; it is not something that is hidden. The bigger problem is that nobody ever addresses it.
>
> (Jerald Bush, senior)

> Whiteness in education looks like a teacher calling on a Black student to give their input on slavery. Whiteness in education looks like anytime a topic of slavery or racism occurs, the entire class nervously looks at the Black kid in the room. Whiteness in education looks like creating a lesson plan that takes a month to go over the

American Revolutionary War, and only a few days on the topic of slavery. Whiteness in education looks like only displaying Black history lesson plans in the month of February. Our school systems should not be like this. Our school systems and lesson plans should educate children of all races about the torture and oppression that Black people have been enduring since the beginning of time. In school Black kids should not have to feel uncomfortable during Black history lesson plans, because white kids cannot handle the topic, and nervously watch the Black kids. It is not Black children's job to help white classmates or white teachers feel comfortable with these topics. These are uncomfortable topics that have to be heard and listened to. The school system has to adapt and educate to make these changes happen.

(Sterling Smith, sophomore)

Members of any school organization need to spend time identifying the manifestations of whiteness within their institution. Educators need to question the why behind exclusionary policies, curriculum adoption, and the lack of racial representation—whether staff or students—within institutions. When I worked in a DEI role in a predominately white school district, I often challenged people within antiracist training sessions to think about the shaping of the community. Segregated communities do not happen coincidentally, and their roots typically trace back to historical redlining, housing discrimination, and other forms of structural racism. Love (2019) reminds us that "education research is crowded with studies that acknowledge dark children's pain, but never the source of their pain, the legacy that pain has left, or how that pain can be healed" (p. 13). We need to uncover the source and restructure schools as healing spaces that incorporate equitable systems to support the cultures, identities, and strengths of all learners—*all meaning all* (Figure 1.2).

Whiteness in Education	
This chart demonstrates where whiteness exists in educational spaces and how it manifests.	
Where whiteness resides	**How whiteness shows up**
	Examples of whiteness in education
Disposition, beliefs, and actions Whiteness can manifest in our beliefs and the ways we see as well as respond to students. It can embed stereotypical images, deficit and racist ideologies, and narrow-minded perspectives in our thought process while working with racially, ethnically, and linguistically diverse learners.	Students can sense when their identities, familial structures, contributions, and living experiences are discounted within a learning environment. When we do not critically examine our biases, there is the potential of harming students with our actions and language such as the examples below: • Making students and their families the scapegoats for racial disparities, rather than looking within or evaluating school systems. • Using deficit or coded language (e.g., *"those kids," "inner city," "free and reduced kids,"* etc.). • Projection of racial stereotypes. • Upholding falsehoods of Americanization (i.e., *"If you live in the United States, you must embrace the American way."*). • Providing nicknames to ethnically, linguistically, and racially diverse students rather than pronouncing names correctly • Avoiding conversations about race due to discomfort or potential backlash—who or what are you protecting with your silence?
Curriculum Whiteness can show up in the form of erasure, eliminating the narratives that reflect the histories, stories, and experiences of people of color in curriculum.	• Required texts in units of study that do not mirror the experiences of students of color. • Mentor texts or curricular materials that incorporate stereotypical images or dehumanizing language. • The literary canon when used as a standard for literacy instruction, omitting authors of color and lived experiences of communities of color. • History texts that highlight the oppression of people of color and not the stories of joy, wonder, and resistance as a strength. • Centering of the English language, erasing the native languages of students in instructional experiences.
Policies Whiteness can appear in the policies that govern schools that do not take the identities of students of color into consideration.	• Criminalization of Black and Brown students with discipline policies (i.e., *dress codes, hairstyles, headwear, etc.*).
Partnerships The partnerships that we devise may uphold whiteness and operate with a lens that lacks racial equity. We must vet the partners we allow in educational spaces to work with students and families.	• Utilizing agencies that do not center voices of color in effort to support marginalized communities (i.e., *agencies "committed" to diversity and inclusion with a lack of racial representation or depth of knowledge of DEI work within their own organizations*). • Community engagement opportunities that are exclusionary to families of color.
Calendars Whiteness can be revealed through what we acknowledge and celebrate.	• Themed weeks where featured events marginalize students (e.g.,*themes that encourage cultural appropriation*). • Disregarding the cultural and religious observances of racially, ethnically, and culturally diverse learners.

FIGURE 1.2 Whiteness in Education

Reimagining Education Outside the Confines of Whiteness

When I think about the structural layout and designs of classroom environments, curriculum, and policies of education, I cannot help but reflect on how different American schools would be if their foundations were not adhered to whiteness. I often think about the collectivism demonstrated in Indigenous communities and how education would have evolved without the entanglement of white supremacy; to build pedagogical sites steeped in the strengths of Indigenous culture where reciprocity between humans, language, land, and experiences were considered as powerful components of a society's sustainability. What would schools look like if the current political structures were not formed through a history of assimilationist, racist ideologies that made the cultures outside of the dominant invisible and promulgated erasure? How different would the experiences of children be if each school environment embraced the central tenet of the Lakota Nation, *"Mitakuye Oyasin,"* emphasizing the power of integrative and inclusive communities (Cajete, 2013) where the notion exists that we are all connected and tied together?

My mind also drifts to the Black literary societies of the 1800s that Gholdy Muhammad (2020) beautifully resurfaced in *Cultivating Genius*, and their preservation if the power dynamics of a racialized society were not in place. I reimagine the outcomes of *Brown vs. Board* (1954) and its impact on children of color while thinking about the following questions:

- ◆ What if white students integrated into predominantly Black schools following the *Brown vs. Board* (1954) ruling?
- ◆ What would the landscape of education look like if the 38,000 Black educators who lost their positions following *Brown vs. Board* (1954) were able to maintain their careers?
- ◆ What if teachers were required to engage in comprehensive identity work and practice anti-bias, antiracist pedagogy before working with children?
- ◆ What if literature authored by people of color were required texts and courses in educational spaces?
- ◆ What if schools highlighted the joy and strengths of people of color in curriculum and did not center stories of oppression?

- ◆ What if all schools honored the native languages of students or AAVE (African American Vernacular English)?
- ◆ What if schools upheld systems that affirmed identities instead of erased?

Imagine an educational system where all educators teach with a critical consciousness, growth mindset, and commit to mirror work for personal development. *Imagine* if students could show up authentically in classrooms anchored in love for their humanity. *Imagine* the beloved communities educators could co-construct with students if responsive to their basic needs and human rights. *Imagine* the barriers we could remove if we organized and mobilized people outside of our institutions to lobby against policies that uphold systemic racism. *Imagine* if we—*looking more so at white people as data is readily available*—voted for leaders invested in the freedom for all people. *Imagine* the cross-cultural healing and empathy that could emerge from the releasing of trauma and falsehoods internalized about race. Let's release, heal, rebuild, and breathe in restoration.

Culturally Responsive Teaching

Culture describes the pattern of human behavior that includes the customs, beliefs, language, and values of a racial, ethnic, religious, or social group. The brain uses cultural information to create meaning from our experiences. Culture shapes our thinking and the ways we network or respond to groups or individuals. Since culture influences how we encode new information, it is a critical factor of learning. Therefore, an identity affirming space is an environment that acknowledges and validates the cultural experiences of learners.

Zaretta Hammond's (2015) neuroscience research conveyed that culture is software for the brain's hardware. The brain makes sense of the world through the behavioral patterns of culture. Hammond (2015) describes three levels of culture in *Culturally Responsive Teaching and the Brain* (pp. 22–23):

Surface culture: the observable and tangible elements of including attire, food, music, and celebrations.

Shallow culture: the unspoken rules surround social norms, interactions, and experiences, including but not limited to rules about eye contact, personal space, concept of time, and nonverbal communication.

Deep culture: the unconscious assumptions that direct the ways we see the world that may include spirituality, theories, ethics, or health.

Oftentimes, educational spaces focus on the surface level of culture. Paul Gorski's (2019) publication *Taco Night* describes how he attended a school event as a student that was annually scheduled near Cinco de Mayo. The celebration included colorful decorations, piñatas, tacos, and music. However, the event did allow anyone to walk away knowing the rich history or contributions of Mexican Americans nor the purpose of Cinco de Mayo. As the wife of a Mexican American, I guarantee the celebration did not likely have authentic tacos either—*something I learned while dating my husband who was initially disappointed by my Americanized concept of a taco.* The cosmetic approaches to honoring culture are also dismissive of the struggles and inequities marginalized communities encounter (e.g., *celebrating Cinco de Mayo while never acknowledging the horrors and separation of families at the US–Mexico border*). The observable and tangible elements of culture do not necessarily capture the ways one defines their individuality, and as educators, there's a need to be conscientious of these levels of culture and the qualities assigned to people based on our understanding of cultural identities.

As multicultural education materialized in the 1970s to combat institutional discrimination, methods were devised to honor the cultural strengths of learners and eradicate assimilationist ideologies in school (Gollnick & Chinn, 1998). Gloria Ladson-Billings and Geneva Gay paved the way for educators to think about the framework of culturally relevant and responsive teaching practices. Culturally responsive teaching legitimizes the histories of racial and ethnic identities and challenges structures that marginalize students. Learning becomes more meaningful in the eyes of children when individualized strengths are affirmed and validated within the classroom environment.

Culturally responsive teaching uses the lived experiences of students as a foundation to build knowledge and skills (Murff, 2020). It requires educators to be warm demanders (Gay, 2000) who demonstrate a caring demeanor with students while maintaining high expectations and providing clear guidance to accelerate growth. Importantly, culturally responsive educators serve as a bridge between schools and communities. They build partnerships and effectively communicate with students, families, and other various stakeholder groups that support schools.

Educators who embrace and implement culturally responsive teaching commit to the following practices:

1. *Engage in an ongoing process of self-examination to monitor biases and ideologies.* The notion does not exist that one has already learned what they need to know. Rather, educators position themselves to understand cultural perspectives and values outside of their own.

2. *Learn how to validate and affirm the cultural identities of learners,* using knowledge learned to support instructional practices and helping students to see a positive image of self. Differences (e.g., *linguistic, cultural, racial, ability, ethnic, gender, etc.*) are viewed as strengths.

3. *Actively removes the barriers* that hinder the success of students, including forms of oppression to ensure educational equity for all. This requires an understanding of the sociopolitical contexts that affect students' navigation in society.

4. *Use data, student voice, and community input to drive school-based decisions.* This work is results-oriented, and equity is activated when we place students as well as families in the center of decisions that impact educational experiences.

5. *Ensure that students have access to resources and multiple entry points into learning experiences.* Culture influences how we learn, meaning that the ignition for learning and scaffolds for support will look different for each student.
6. *Hold high expectations for all students.* Children are brilliant, capable, and able to do insightful work. Believe in them. Evaluate systems of support.
7. *Engage in proactive work to support social emotional learning.* Emphasize the importance of self-awareness and emotional wellness. Create environments that allow for students to be their authentic selves in a space that enhances their intellectual capacity.

As a school administrator, I also believe that educational leaders play a critical role in generating an environment that encourages teachers to understand, practice, and improve instructional skills to meet the diverse needs of learners. Teachers should feel supported to embrace new approaches and grow in areas of culturally responsive pedagogy. There should also be accountability measures in place to monitor the effectiveness of strategies and guide instruction. I recommend that district and building level leaders actively practice the considerations below, while teachers use this guidance as a reflection tool to assess leadership and whether their environment will support the work of creating an affirming space. Here are considerations for school administrators:

1. *Critically examine your own identity and how it influences leadership.* How does your social construction shape the way you lead? Is there a connection between the way you were conditioned to understand differences and how you respond to people within your school community, including staff? Engage in self work to build a critical consciousness and knowledge about equitable practices.
2. *Build a common language for educational equity and cultural responsivity among staff.* Ensure that every staff member understands educational equity in action, mirror work, and strategies that are culturally responsive.

3. *Model mirror work and vulnerability.* It is hard to follow someone who uses all the buzzwords but does not make the work of equity visible in their own life.

4. *Understand the power dynamics, including your own, that may hinder the progression of equitable spaces.* Humans in positions of power create policies and systems, thus, they have the ability to change and dismantle oppressive structures too. The question is, *do you have the will to do the work?*

5. *Create spaces for professional learning and debriefing.* Provide time for teachers to not only learn pedagogical approaches, but to grapple with how to put theory into practice.

6. *Critically examine systems to assess structures of support for learners.* Study systems and conditions for learning. Help staff to think about the existence of inequities within professional learning communities and organize to disrupt the status quo.

7. *Evaluate school climate and culture through the voices of staff, students, and families.* Consider the voices that are being centered in decision-making processes, initiatives, and think about who is impacted.

8. *Work closely with community stakeholders to understand needs and share progress of measures toward equitable outcomes.* Focus on the development of learning partnerships and how information is cascaded in accessible ways throughout a community.

The next chapter will focus on the concept of educational equity. It is essential for educators to understand the components of equitable environments, the power dynamics involved, and how we provide access to educational resources. Educational equity is a process that involves one's will to change practices that contribute to marginalization and unequal outcomes. It requires a critical mass of people to come together to collaborate, problem-solve, and hold each other accountable as an act of love.

Chapter Highlights

- ◆ The classroom is an impactful factor of identity development and student learning.
- ◆ Education is political. Full stop.
- ◆ Educators must understand the sociopolitical contexts and the connections between identity and societal systems.
- ◆ An identity affirming space cannot exist in absence of anti-bias, antiracist work where we identify forms of oppression within schools and decenter whiteness.
- ◆ Educators—teachers and administrators—need to embrace cultural responsivity and recognize that the cultural identities of students serve as a foundation to build skills and knowledge.

 Collective Work: Identifying How Whiteness Shows Up

Whether in a professional learning community, grade level team planning session, or during a time of collaboration with colleagues, get into a critical dialogue and think about the ways whiteness shows up in school environments. Reflect on the curriculum, policies, calendars and schedules, and the aspects of your school culture. After identifying the manifestations of whiteness within your institution, interrogate why it exists. The next chapter will discuss the disruption process and provide more tools for framing your thinking. However, the intent of this exercise is for you to normalize naming racial inequities. Talk about race in clear ways, eliminating coded language. Before we can disrupt, we must name what is problematic. Let's name, then develop a plan of action. The following chapter will also help you to think about systematic cultural shifts (Figure 1.3).

Whiteness in Education Understanding where whiteness exists in educational spaces and how it manifests		
Educational spaces *Identifying where whiteness is evident.*	**How whiteness shows up** *Think about the ways whiteness is evident in your classroom/school environment. Use the reflective questions to help guide thoughts.*	**Decentering whiteness** *What strategies can you use to address what you have identified?*
Disposition, beliefs, and actions Whiteness can manifest in our beliefs and the ways we see as well as respond to students. It can embed stereotypical images, deficit and racist ideologies, and narrow-minded perspectives in our thought process while working with racially, ethnically, and linguistically diverse learners.	Reflective Qs: *Review data. What story does it convey?* *When discussing students at the margins in grade level planning meetings does more asset-based or deficit language emerge?*	
Curriculum Whiteness can show up in the form of erasure, eliminating the narratives that reflect the histories, stories, and experiences of people of color in curriculum.	Reflective Qs: *Whose voices are centered in instructional materials? How are the lives, stories, and histories of people of color validated?*	
Policies Whiteness can appear in the policies that govern schools that do not take the cultural identities of students of color into consideration.	Reflective Qs: *Who benefits from policies and practices that are in place within the classroom or school? Who is harmed by those same policies and practices?*	
Partnerships The partnerships that we devise may uphold whiteness and operate with a lens that lacks racial equity. We must vet the partners we allow in educational spaces.	Reflective Qs: *How do organizations work in community with people of color? Are decisions made for marginalized communities or with their input and leadership?*	
Calendars Whiteness can be revealed through what we acknowledge and celebrate.	Reflective Qs: *What do you celebrate in school (i.e., holidays, themed days, etc.)? Do you consider religious and cultural observances before planning events to ensure no one is automatically excluded?*	

FIGURE 1.3 Decentering Whiteness

References

Aguilar, E. (2020). *Coaching for Equity.* Hoboken, NJ: Jossey-Bass.

Buchanan-Rivera, E. (2019, October 24). *Identity-Affirming Classrooms Need Race-Conscious Teachers.* ASCD. www.ascd.org/ascd-express/

vol15/num04/identity-affirming-schools-need-race-conscious-educators.aspx

Cajete, G. (2015). *Indigenous Community: Rekindling the Teachings of the Seventh Fire*. St. Paul, MN: Living Justice Press.

Delgado, Richard, & Stefancic, Jean. (2001). *The Critical Race Theory: An Introduction*. New York, NY: New York University Press.

Dunbar-Ortiz, R. (2015). *An Indigenous Peoples' History of the United States*. Boston, MA: Beacon Press.

Gay, Geneva. (2000). *Culturally Responsive Teaching: Theory, Research, and Practice*. New York, NY: Teachers College Press.

Gollnick, D., & Chinn, P. (1998). *Multicultural Education in a Pluralistic Society* (5th ed.). Upper Saddle River, NJ: Merrill.

Gorski, P. (2019, October 7). Taco night. *EdChange*. http://edchange.org/publications/TacoNight.pdf

Hamlin, A. D. F. (Ed.) (1910). *Modern School Houses: Being a Series of Authoritative Articles on Planning, Sanitation, Heating and Ventilation* (Vol. 1). New York, NY: Swetland Publishing Company.

Hammond, Z. (2015). *Culturally Responsive Teaching and the Brain*. Thousand Oaks, CA: Corwin.

Harris, C.I. (1993). Whiteness as property. *Harvard Law Review*, *106*(8), 1707–1791.

Hille, R.T. (2011). *Modern Schools: A Century of Design for Education*. Hoboken, NJ: Wiley and Sons.

Horton, J.O., & Horton, L.E. (2001). *Hard Road to Freedom: The Story of African America*. New Brunswick, NJ: Rutgers University Press.

Jones, D., & Hagopian, J. (Eds.). (2020). *An Uprising for Educational Justice: Black Lives Matter at School*. Chicago, IL: Haymarket Books.

Kimmerer, Robin W. (2013). *Braiding Sweetgrass: Indigenous Wisdom, Scientific Knowledge, and the Teachings of Plants*. Minneapolis, MN: Milkweed Editions.

Kirst, M.W., & Wirt, F.M. (2009). *The Political Dynamics of American Education* (4th ed.). Richmond, CA: McCutchan Publishing Co.

Ladson-Billings, Gloria. (1994). *The Dreamkeepers: Successful Teachers of African American Children*. San Francisco, CA: John Wiley & Sons.

Love, B. (2019). *We want to do More than Survive*. Boston, MA: Beacon Press.

Lutz, Mallory. (2017). The hidden cost of Brown v. Board: African American educators' resistance to desegregating schools. *Online Journal of Rural Research & Policy, 12*(4). doi:10.4148/1936-0487.1085

Lyiscott, J. (2019). *Black Appetite, White Food*. New York, NY: Routledge.

McHenry, E. (2002). *Forgotten Readers: Recovering the Lost History of African American Literacy Societies*. Durham, NC: Duke University Press.

Minow, M. (2010). *In Brown's Wake*. New York, NY: Oxford University Press.

Muhammad, G. (2020). *Cultivating Genius: An Equity Framework for Culturally and Historically Responsive Literacy*. New York, NY: Scholastic.

Murff, D. (2020). *Culturally Responsive Pedagogy: Promising Practices for African American Male Students*. Charlotte, NC: Information Age Publishing.

Nieto, S., & Bode, P. (2017). *Affirming Diversity: The Sociopolitical Context of Multicultural Education* (7th ed.). New York, NY: Pearson.

Pai, Y., Adler, S.A., & Shadiow, L.K. (2006). *Cultural Foundations of Education* (4th ed.). Upper Saddle River, NJ: Merrill Prentice Hall.

Shalaby, C. (2017). *Troublemakers: Lessons in Freedom from Young Children in School*. New York, NY: The New Press.

Singh, A. (2019). *Racial Healing Handbook: Practical Activities to Help You Challenge Privilege, Confront Systemic Racism, and Engage in Collective Healing*. Oakland, CA: New Harbinger Publications, Inc.

Theoharis, J. (2018). *A More Beautiful and Terrible History*. Boston, MA: Beacon Press.

Urban, W.J., & Wagoner, J.L. (2014). *American Education: A History* (5th ed.). New York, NY: Routledge.

Weisser, A.S. (2006, August). Little red school house, what now? Two centuries of American public school architecture. *Journal of Planning History, 5*(3), 196.

Wilkerson, I. (2020). *Caste*. New York, NY: Random House.

2

Leading for Equity

In order for all students to experience educational excellence, there must be equity of access, resources, content, and processes.

Geneva Gay (1994, p. 126)

We live in a society where people seek an antidote for multilayered problems.

Creating equitable, just communities is contingent upon a systematic removal of barriers and the sharing of power. You cannot serve a community if you are not *in community* with people, learning from their experiences and listening to their needs. This is human work. The labor is complex and messy, but we're the ones we've been waiting for. We can move in solidarity together if we have the will.

> The oppressive structures in educational systems will not disband with technical changes, but with deep cultural shifts that involve us seeing ourselves and how we uphold the status quo.

What is Equity?

Educational systems were not designed to generate equal outcomes or opportunities for everyone. The work of building

DOI: 10.4324/9781003216964-4

identity affirming spaces is reliant upon a foundation of equity and collectivist approaches. In the field of education, equity is the concept of giving individuals what they need to thrive, which requires an elimination of oppressive structures and methods of subjugation that particularly harm marginalized communities. Within an equitable institution, one should not be able to predict outcomes based on how students identify.

To advance educational equity, we must ensure that students from all backgrounds have access to opportunities and resources that support intellectual as well as social-emotional needs. Geneva Gay (1994) explained, in *At the Essence of Learning: Multicultural Education*, that students need equity of access, resources, content, and processes to experience educational excellence. Behind the creation of every system are human beings. When actions are led by biases, deficit ideologies, and limited knowledge about culture, systems will continue to exclude as historically designed. Therefore, the grind of changing and rebuilding systems must accompany mirror work. It requires the development of culturally responsive educators who continuously examine their biases, positionality, and sociopolitical contexts in efforts to build authentic connections with learners. Equity is not a buzzword, yet an action that involves lifelong, intergenerational work and a redistribution of power to underserved communities.

While serving as a principal, I strived to be the leader I needed for myself within school experiences. As a survivor of institutional trauma, I wanted to be a part of the development of a culture where all students felt visible. The school I served had a large population of multilingual learners due to a redistricting process where boundaries were changed for enrollment. Teachers could feel the shift in demographics, frustrated by the lack of resources and personnel to support diverse, linguistic needs. Many struggled to find effective ways to communicate with multilingual families. The story of transformational work began with spaces for listening and learning.

Teachers were immersed in professional learning experiences that centered belief systems about children and their capabilities. I curated a series of sessions that focused on pedagogical approaches to support multilingual learners in partnership with my alma mater, Butler University. Collectively as a staff, we developed a School Community Council that incorporated local agencies, religious institutions, and businesses that met with the purpose of building a bridge between the school and community. Through community focus groups and events designed for multilingual families, we identified specific needs and developed a grant proposal that secured nearly $400,000 for after-school bilingual support services as well as an adult English education program. This school, which reflected pockets of areas challenged with poverty and crime, became an A-rated, nationally recognized magnet school due to the will of staff who listened to the voices of families and prioritized their needs. (*Note: We can hold multiple truths. I celebrate the work of educators supporting the needs of students and recognize that accountability metrics on a state level are inherently inequitable too.*)

Equity centered leadership, whether serving as a teacher or an administrator, involves a critical examination of systems. We give ourselves permission to let go of practices that do not work for all learners. Brooklyn-based educator and author Cornelius Minor has often conveyed that "we can abandon yesterday's ideas, if they don't serve today's needs." We do not have to emulate pedagogies from our past or tether ourselves to pacing guides absent of humanizing content and foundational skills. Submission to an inequitable system won't change outcomes. Rather, it's about positioning ourselves to combat inequities through the use of critical questions, intercultural dialogue, and impactful actions that disrupt the status quo. Educators leading for equity exemplify the following qualities in within their school community while working with students, families, and colleagues:

Systems-focused: Makes a deliberative effort to transform systems and dismantle institutional oppression. One identifies existing inequities, barriers that prohibit equitable results, and strategies for cultural shifts or structural changes.

Critical examiner: Cultivates a lens of criticality to examine systems and conditions for learning. One evaluates systems to determine the causes of outcomes, rather than positioning students or caregivers as the scapegoats for inequalities.

Disruptor: Challenges the status quo and says what needs to be said in the moment. One is not desensitized to the identity threats students (or staff) encounter and disrupts rhetoric or practices that are damaging to children (or colleagues).

Upholds accountability: Holds self and others accountable as an act of love. One recognizes that a cohesive, unified community cannot exist without compassion and justice.

Mindful communicator: Listens to the needs of a community (e.g., *students, families, colleagues, etc.*) and seeks to understand diverse perspectives. One is conscientious of voices that are centered and works to ensure that all students feel valued for their contributions.

Builds community: Fosters a sense of belonging and connectivity. One strives to build authentic relationships with learners with an awareness that support looks different to every student.

Leading for Equity

Leadership matters. Power dynamics within school environments determine the progression of educational equity. As a consultant and DEI director, I have worked with numerous teachers who have not felt empowered to engage in transformative work due to leadership. Teachers have shared that school administrators (board members too) may stifle efforts to advance equity to avoid conflict or community backlash. We must question the voices that are centered in decisions that impact educational experiences. When decisions cater to people's discomfort with ideals of equity, no one becomes free. Liberatory work and the restructuring of educational systems to create identity affirming spaces are going to come with risks (e.g., *disgruntled people, resistance, loss of relationships, safety, etc.*), yet there must be a commitment to work through the road-blocks with the shield and power of community. Although this book heavily focuses on teachers, I need to be clear that they cannot be the only educators moving the needle toward equity. Everyone plays a part and decisions that are made by educational leaders (e.g., *superintendents, principals, school board members, directors, etc.*) directly influence experiences in classroom environments.

To white educators, it's important to acknowledge the privilege that is connected to your identity and examine the power dynamics within an institution. Think about the voices you lift to guide equitable practices and how you measure outcomes. *Do you actively listen to the needs of underserved groups, including colleagues of color? How have the voices of marginalized communities shaped your practices and pedagogical shifts?* The work of advancing equity requires self-introspection and active listening that leads to action. If you teach in a predominantly white community, it is especially important to think about the knowledge students need to combat inequities as a part of this generational work. Normalize conversations about identity, humanity, and race. Being a part of the change and leading for equity calls for all of us to be critical examiners of ourselves and the systems developed to support the communities we serve.

To educators of color, it's necessary for me to racialize my voice here. As a Black woman, I recognize that the work of educational equity can be tiresome for those who do not proximate their identity to whiteness. We cannot escape the harm of oppressive environments in our lived experiences while showing up for work and challenging a system that was not built for our existence. Racial trauma wears on our health and emotional wellness. The work within the field of education is endless, and as someone who wants you to thrive, I encourage you to seek spaces where your contributions are valued. We also need to find effective ways to combat racial battle fatigue (Smith, Hung, & Franklin, 2011) and develop healing spaces. There have been times when racial trauma has consumed my life and negatively affected my physical health. We must remember to breathe deeply in this work, lean on communities of care, and identify the support that we need. I will also reiterate that there is mirror work for us to do in efforts to decenter internalized whiteness consumed from school and/or life experiences.

To curriculum directors or instructional coaches, leading for equity entails an evaluation of curricular materials and pedagogical approaches. It is important to name the cultural perspectives that are dominant and missing within the curriculum. Rudine Sims Bishop (1990) uplifts the concept of windows and mirrors in literacy. Students need an opportunity to see their identities reflected in texts (mirror) and a space to learn about lived experience outside of their own (window). In efforts of creating an identity affirming space, curriculum directors must be aware of content that contributes to negative typecasts of racial groups or problematic ideologies that threaten one's identity. A process for evaluating biases in texts could be a proactive tool for educators.

The incorporation of linguistic and gender diversity in curriculum should also be elevated. Students need access to texts that honor their native language and culture. The provision of culturally responsive curricular resources or inclusive libraries does not equate to one's ability to engage in a productive conversation about humanity. As a former director of curriculum, I would typically engage administrators and teachers in thoughtfully crafted simulations to enhance their knowledge base, strategies for critical conversations, and pedagogical approaches. Provide time for administrators and teachers to learn, debrief, and collaborate. Educational leaders and teachers need enriched learning experiences yet must have space and time to process new understandings.

To school administrators, the creation of equitable schools is contingent upon your investment in the work and the ways you support educators who are empowered to disrupt oppressive structures. I have worked with hundreds of educators who feel like they're in a complicated relationship with their institutions due to administrators whose actions negate their proclaimed beliefs about equity. Dedicate time for self-work where you learn how to identify biases and microaggressions as we have all breathed in stereotypical images and language. Make your beliefs about equity visible. Provide encouragement to teachers who are committed to employing culturally responsive teaching practices, antiracism work, and transforming systems. Teachers who are on fire for devising affirming spaces do not want to operate under performative leadership. You are setting the tone and vision for the work and must lead by example.

To DEI officers or directors, work in a corporation or district where leaders from the school board to superintendents demonstrate a strong commitment to equity work. You are not hired to check anyone's box and need to have the autonomy to engage in a process of disruption. Raise critical questions and challenge the status quo. Make sure that you're in a place that values your input and speak truth to power. Educational equity requires collective work and should not fall on the shoulders of one person. If you find yourself in a position where you are the sole voice and problem-solver for everything DEI related, you may need to question the principles of leaders- *who hired you to do a specific job-* and consider a change.

In my experience and networks, many DEI positions are filled largely by women of color who are placed in a role to dismantle an impenetrable system of whiteness. I have been a DEI officer in a predominantly white institution as the only Black woman in a central office position. This work will come with significant challenges and perils. You are not there to help students and staff cope with the harsh realities of inequities. Rather, you are there to eradicate inequities, barriers, and policies that marginalize students. In this line of work, backlash and resistance are inevitable yet continue to move forward in the name of humanity and protect your peace when possible along the way. You are needed and the work matters.

Disrupting Inequities

The development of equitable systems requires a disruption of harmful structures and practices. This work is nurtured through collectivism, necessitating a community of people working together. The following outlines a framework for consideration. Mirror work is always a powerful first and ongoing step, followed by the formation of accountability partners, the identification and interrogation of inequities, and the disrupting structures or systems of oppression. Lisa Delpit reminds us that we do not really "see through our eyes and ears, but through our beliefs" (2006, p. 46). Therefore, commitment to self-work and the cultivation of a critical consciousness help to guide the work.

Find Your People

In an ideal world, every educator would commit to justice-centered work in classrooms. There would be an insatiable desire to shift traditional pedagogies that do not foster meaningful experiences for students or accelerate learning. However, individualized beliefs about equitable practices are filtered through a lens of cultural experiences. The history of liberatory work entails oppressors who fought (and still fight) to maintain power, and educational environments are no different when people in varied capacities fight to uphold unjust conditions.

Through community, we learn how to organize and navigate tensions. We all need people, particularly colleagues, who will challenge our thinking, vocalize truths, and hold us accountable. Seek people, whether in or outside of your institution (e.g., via conferences, social media, equity-focused organizations), who will support your journey of becoming a better human. Surround yourself with individuals who have the endurance and strength to combat the status quo when it does not support all students. Find your people and stay connected to a community that will enrich your life and mindset with new perspectives.

Identify and Interrogate Inequities

We cannot develop equitable solutions if we refuse to name the problems that plague our institutions. *If curriculum and pedagogical approaches are not benefiting all students*, an audit of instructional delivery and content, classroom culture, and assessments can determine strengths, malpractices, and areas for improvement. *If students with disabilities are not receiving appropriate accommodations*, the breakdowns within systems of support, communication, and assessments need to be analyzed. *If achievement disparities are based on grading practices*, then policies need an examination, hopefully, leading to an entirely different model for reporting academic progress and representations of learning.

We must name inequities. When inequities are identified, we can begin to eliminate the patterns that perpetuate disparities. Bryan Stevenson (2020), attorney and founder of the Equal Justice Initiative, says that we have to get proximate to problems and understand the nature of how they operate. We have a responsibility to

> The disruption process for the shaping of equitable school communities starts when we acknowledge what sabotages learning outcomes.

interrogate what is not working and examine the functionality of our systems, questioning why the inequities exist. Knowing the source can inform us of strategies for disruption.

Listen, Don't Exploit

The measuring stick for equitable environments should be based on the considerations and perspectives of people at the margins. Instead of making decisions *for* the benefit of underserved communities, a sharing of power is needed to position marginalized groups as leaders within the process of transformative work. Listening spaces, as described in Chapter 5, allow room for the stories of families and students who have been disenfranchised by systems and decisions made within institutions. For example, how often do you ask students what can be improved to enhance learning or increase levels of engagement? Do students of all ages have the opportunity to share objectives learned and ask questions when lessons are misunderstood? While adults are elevating the notion of "learning loss" in the context of the COVID-19 global pandemic, what counter-narratives have emerged from students regarding what they have gained? What platforms have been created for families to share information about their students' experiences? Although listening tours are valuable, it's imperative to note that no one owes us their story. When students and families share their experiences and trauma, it is with the hope that people will respond and initiate organizational changes—after all, this is equity work, not exploitation. We need to listen and act.

Reimagine, Eradicate, and Rebuild

Think about the oppressive structures that were identified in listening spaces and the multiple perspectives collected throughout the process. *How would the system(s) operate without the existence of inequities? What would the system look and feel like to students? What strategies could be developed to eradicate the barriers?* Get in the mindset of liberation. Start outlining the action steps that are necessary to remove obstacles. *What resources are needed to rebuild systems? Will those resources require funding?* This work is not prescriptive; however, it is helpful to use data (e.g., quantitative, and qualitative) and research to guide efforts. If the current systems are not generating equitable outcomes, there's no reason to maintain them. It's beyond time to release the *"we've always done it that way"* excuse and unravel traditional, cultural school norms that are detrimental to students.

Working through power dynamics where specific leaders or school boards are barriers to educational equity can be an intricate process. I have worked in districts with school board members who were openly homophobic, classist, and racist, which significantly impacted policy decisions. The organizing of communities can be an influential factor in disrupting power structures. I have mobilized communities to advocate for changes within school districts. Communities can unite to push back against systemic inequities, and you can certainly be some of the strings behind that work and evoke change. Again, this work comes with risks.

Setting the Stage for Equitable Environments

Educational equity centers the removal of oppressive environments or malpractices, and the creation of conditions where learners thrive, with a concentrated focus on underserved communities. This chapter has focused heavily on systems work, yet here are some other considerations to keep in mind when restructuring pedagogies and ameliorating school environments to support learners.

Identity Affirmations

There is a strong correlation between learning and the partnerships that exist between students and teachers. James Comer (1995) has conveyed that learning cannot occur without a significant relationship. At the heart of any positive, functional relationship lies trust. Identity affirmations can help to build trust and make students feel emotionally safe. An affirmation refers to the acknowledgment of one's identity and how one conveys care and respect for one's personhood. Equitable environments illustrate culturally responsive practices that recognize the strengths and capabilities of each learner. The emphasis on connections will be expanded upon in Chapter 5.

Racial Consciousness

The critique of liberalism is a CRT tenet that calls for a race-conscious approach in the transformation of systems. This approach must reject colorblind methodologies of neutrality or meritocracy that disregard a student's racial identity and experiences while operating in inequitable systems (Gillborn & Ladson-Billings, 2010). The colorblind concept is guised as a form of equality, imbued in the notion that naming differences is problematic (Milner & Ross, 2006). It is used to justify inaction in addressing racial disparities, which perpetuates the permeance of systemic and institutionalized racism (Wise, 2010). When we assert that we see all students as the same, we dehumanize and discount their experiences, perspectives, and identities (Buchanan-Rivera, 2019). As my friend and educational author, Rosa Perez-Isiah (Isiah, 2020) would say, we need to focus on the creation of color-brave spaces where we examine racial biases and normalize conversations about race.

Access and Opportunities

Students should have equal access and opportunities to excel within school environments. The pathways and level of support may look different for each student, yet opportunities should be accessible to all. As a part of the disruption process, we need to identify access and opportunity gaps, questioning the source of the disparity. I have worked with schools where students lacked the opportunity to join specialized courses (e.g., *art, band, orchestra, etc.*) due to assigned remedial classes based on course or standardized assessments. Another example relevant to my experiences includes students lacking access to hot lunches due to delinquent account balances which is completely out of the child's control. The *Boston Globe* reported in 2017 that 15-year-old twin, Black students received detentions for wearing braided hair extensions (Lazar, 2017). The hairstyle went against Mystic Valley Regional's Charter School's policy which was reportedly developed in the name of educational equity. Sometimes school policies do not allow for students to reach their full potential, causing isolation and hindering growth. And note, that if a policy marginalizes students, it's not equitable.

Intent vs. Impact

As educators we must recognize that good intentions do not automatically lead to equitable outcomes. We can have beautiful thoughts and objectives for creating an affirming space, yet what matters is our impact. Equitable outcomes require intentional actions. One of the Black Student Union organizations (BSU) that I supported as a DEI officer, hosted an annual gathering to present racial equity progress and concerns to faculty and staff. During my last year working within that school corporation, members of BSU decided to invite participants (teachers and administrators) by invitation only. When I asked the students why they did not extend an invite to other administrators (e.g., superintendents, directors, etc.), the reply was *"We only invited people who will actually listen."*

Students are watching to see who leads inclusively and for equity. Words are powerful when they are backed by our actions.

If we assert beliefs about equity, they must be aligned with intentional actions in an environment (climate, conditions, and physical space) that supports culturally responsive practices. The following chart helps us to think about the alignment between our beliefs, actions, and the environments we create for students. How are we moving beyond our beliefs and are we thinking about the systems as well as environments that will uphold them? (Figure 2.1)

> How many years will we talk about our intentions before students feel the impact of change?

Beliefs	Actions	Environment
What are my beliefs about teaching? What are my beliefs about students? What are my beliefs about diversity, equity, and inclusion? What do I believe about antiracist work?	**What actions support my beliefs? What does the following say about my beliefs?** ▪ Data (e.g., achievement, discipline, etc.) ▪ Curriculum ▪ Policies ▪ Hiring practices (for administrators)	Have I constructed an environment that supports my actions and beliefs?
Example of alignment reflection Note: *Evidence is key. How do you know the impact of your actions?*		
Black lives matter.	Continually examine racial biases. Center **Black excellence** in curriculum. Publicly acknowledge how anti-Black racism is evident in systems and unite others to act. Address policies that marginalize Black students.	Create spaces that validate the lived experiences of Black students as evidenced by student and caregiver feedback, curricular materials, features in physical environment, etc.
There's power in student voice.	Create ongoing opportunities for students to share their thinking and learning experiences. Student feedback continually informs instructional practices (e.g., surveys, exit tickets, etc.). Build a collaborative community where students learn through interactive dialogues.	Use the expressions of students to design the layout and classroom environment as evidenced by representations of learning and physical features that are relevant and meaningful to students.

FIGURE 2.1 The Alignment of Beliefs, Actions, and Environments

Cultivating an Equity Mindset

The development of an equity lens requires one to immerse oneself in diverse perspectives, making a deliberate effort to seek narratives outside of personal lived experiences. "We must learn to be vulnerable enough to allow our world to turn upside down in order to allow the realities of others to edge themselves into our consciousness" (Delpit, 2006, p. 47). An equity-minded person welcomes opportunities that challenge their worldview and thanks people who have the courage to tell them when they've made a mistake. When approaching the disruption process with an equity mindset, think about the following questions:

1. What systems within the institution generate inequitable outcomes?
2. Which identity groups benefit or are harmed by the educational systems in place (e.g., race, gender, ability, etc.)?
3. Does my commitment to equity reflect intersectional work, including all identities?
4. Have I considered the sociopolitical contexts that students and families navigate?
5. Whose voices do I center while striving to advance equity?
6. Am I open and willing to learn as well as unlearn?
7. How am I decentering whiteness in education?
8. Do I normalize conversations about race, whiteness, biases (e.g., gender, class, ability, etc.), and humanity?
9. When discussing racial disparities existing in data and developing strategies, how are the voices of communities of color centered?
10. Do I know when to speak and when to hand over the mic in conversations about race, power, and identity?

This is a process of learning and unlearning. Students did not create the inequalities rampant in educational systems. As adults, the heavy lifting is on us and we have work to do.

 **Mirror Work**

Take time to process the following questions independently. This work requires us to think about who we're in community with, the skills we need to develop a critical consciousness, and how we can hold ourselves accountable to growth. In the song "Doo Wop" one of my favorite artists, Lauryn Hill, says, *"How you gonna win when you ain't right within?"* We cannot win in this work of pursuing equity and justice if we fail to address our own stuff. Mirror work can be a healing space that sets us free. Continue to add thoughts from your last journal entry. Get personal.

Social contexts

- What is the make-up (e.g., racial, gender, sexual orientation, etc.) of my inner circles? How do my social contexts influence my beliefs about educational equity? Perhaps, some of these people are your accountability partners.

Skills

- What skills and resources do I need to grow in understanding educational equity?

Systems of accountability

- How can I hold myself accountable in the work of creating equitable environments?
- Who are my accountability partners?

Self-Development Plan

We can engage in equity-related book clubs, webinars, and educational conferences, yet we still have to process new concepts and think through the practical applications of new learning. It may be helpful for you to think about a personal self-development plan in efforts to start your journey of learning and unlearning. It's important to think about the following:

1. Who is providing the learning experience? Are they a credible resource of knowledge on the topic?
2. What have I learned from the experience (e.g., *book study, seminar, etc.*)?
3. What am I still wrestling with?
4. Who can serve as an accountability partner for me? (Note: *An accountability partner can help with the first question if you need to vet the validity of a professional development offering or experience*).
5. What will I implement because of new understandings?
6. When will I employ the new skill?
7. How will I monitor the implementation of new practices?

You can map your thinking through a sketch, chart, or, if you're like me, you can keep a learning journal. Yet, note that transformative work requires us to move from awareness to practice. I'll also reiterate that if you're an administrator, you cannot expect growth in practices if you do not provide the time for teachers to collaborate and reflect. Educators need time, space, and resources to deepen learning connections.

Chapter Highlights

- The work of creating just, identity affirming spaces is contingent upon a foundation of equity and collectivist approaches.
- To advance educational equity, we must ensure that students from all backgrounds have access to opportunities and resources to support intellectual as well as social emotional needs.
- Equity work requires a process of disruption.

- Setting the stage for equitable environments involves racially conscious teachers who affirm the identities of learners, understand intent vs. impact, and provide equal access and opportunities to students.

 Collective Work: Dismantling Inequitable Systems

Engage in a disruption process with colleagues and complete the Systems Work Plan. Here are some guiding steps: (see Figure 2.2).

1. Establish or connect with a critical mass of people (e.g., professional learning community, grade level team, equity team, school improvement team, etc.).
2. Identify inequities in systems including but not limited to curriculum, high ability, discipline, dress code policies, grading practices, special education services, supports for linguistic needs, etc.
3. Interrogate why the inequities exist.
4. Seek multiple perspectives (e.g., focus groups, community panels, parent teacher organizations, survey data, etc.).
5. Reimagine systems and determine strategies that will help in the eradication of barriers. Rebuild structures that support the needs of learners and provide equitable access to resources.

Systems work: naming and eradicating inequities

Equity work requires a critical examination of our systems and conditions for learning. We must think about the practices that are implemented in educational settings through an equity lens, recognizing who benefits or may be harmed by educational structures or systems that are in place. Furthermore, it is important to interrogate the why behind the existence of inequities and get to the root of the barriers that hinder the success of students and an inclusive environment. Identity affirming classrooms necessitate a foundation of equity.

Part I. Identification: naming inequities and structural barriers. List educational inequities as evident via data or information collected through listening spaces with students, staff, and caregivers.

Educational inequity	Unpacking of inequity (description)
1.	
2.	
3.	

Part II. Interrogate. Why do the inequities or structural barriers exist? List the inequities named from the identification process below. Discuss why the inequity exists and document in the space provided. If you do not understand why the inequity persists, list what you can do to learn more.

Educational inequity	Unveiling the why
1.	
2.	
3.	

Part III. Short-term goal. Develop short-term goals with your team. Identify any form of support that is needed to address barriers and generate equitable outcomes.

Short-term goal	
Goal	Identify support
1.	
2.	

FIGURE 2.2 Systems Work Plan

Part IV. Long-term goals. Be clear about the time progress will be assessed and denote who will be a part of the process.

Long-term goals		
Goal	Timeline of goal	Tools/methods to measure progress
1.		
2.		

Part V. Barriers. Name the anticipated or current barriers that stifle the progression of (listed) goals. Be clear about power dynamics, skills needed to address the disparity, etc. Remember, this work cannot be shouldered by one or two people. What do you need collectively as a team and how can you build capacity?

Anticipated or current barriers
1.
2.
3.

Part VII. Strategies for barriers. Name strategies you will use to address and confront barriers. If you are not aware of a strategy to use, think about who can assist in the development process.

Strategies: goals can be achieved through methods or resources below
1.
2.
3.

FIGURE 2.2 (Cont.)

Part VIII. Timeline. Note the strategies and/or action steps that your team will implement. Develop a timeline that works best for your team. Below is an example. Discuss when you will touch base to monitor progress and build capacity. **Note:** The 'work' does not have to be scheduled or formatted in this manner. The purpose is to keep the work moving forward and document accountability measures.

Timeline		
Month	**Strategy/method**	**Process owner(s)**
August		
September		
October		
November		
December		
January		
February		
March		
April		
May		
June		
July		

Part IX: Support. Name the support you need from a school building or district level (e.g., directors, instructional coaches, etc.) to assist with goals, professional learning needs, student-based initiatives, parental or caregiver outreach, etc.

Identifying supports

FIGURE 2.2 (Cont.)

References

Bishop, R. (1990). Mirrors, windows, and sliding glass doors. *Perspectives: Choosing and Using Books for the Classroom, 6*(3), 9–11.

Buchanan-Rivera, E. (2019, October 24). *Identity-Affirming Classrooms Need Race-Conscious Teachers.* ASCD. www.ascd.org/ascd-express/vol15/num04/identity-affirming-schools-need-race-conscious-educators.aspx

Comer, J. (1995). *Lecture given at Education Service Center, Region IV.* Houston, TX.

Delpit, L. (2006). *Other People's Children: Cultural Conflict in the Classroom.* New York, NY: The New Press.

Gay, Geneva. (1994). *At the essence of learning: Multicultural education.* New York, NY: Kappa Delta Pi.

Gillborn, D., & Ladson-Billings, G. (2010). Education and critical race theory. In M.W. Apple, S.J. Ball, & L.A. Gandin (Eds.), *The Routledge International Handbook of the Sociology of Education* (pp. 37–47). New York, NY: Routledge.

Isiah, R. (2020, November). *The Leadership Journey from Color-Blind to Color-Brave.* ASCD. www.ascd.org/publications/newsletters/education_update/nov20/vol62/num11/The_Leadership_Journey_from_Color-Blind_to_Color-Brave.aspx

Lazar, Kay. (2017, May 11). Black Malden charter students punished for wearing braided extensions. *Boston Globe.* www.bostonglobe.com/metro/2017/05/11/black-students-malden-school-who-wear-braids-face-punishment-parents-say/stWDIBSCJhw1zocU-WR1QMP/story.html?p1=Article_Inline_Text_Link

Milner, E., & Ross, W. (Eds.). (2006). *Race, Ethnicity, and Education* (4th ed.). Santa Barbara, CA: Praeger.

Smith, W.A., Hung, M., & Franklin, J.D. (2011). Racial battle fatigue and the miseducation of black men: Racial microaggressions, societal problems, and environmental stress. *The Journal of Negro Education, 80*(1), 63–82.

Stevenson, Bryan. (2020, October 25). *Anchorpoint with Bryan Stevenson.* [Virtual lecture]. www.facebook.com/stlukesindy/videos/anchorpoint-w-bryan-stevenson-special-time-830am/352050802521784/

Wise, Tim. (2010). *Colorblind: The Rise of Post-Racial Politics and the Retreat from Racial Equity.* San Francisco, CA: City Lights Books.

Part II

Components of Identity Affirming Spaces

This section will focus on components from my research that help to promote identity affirming educational spaces. As expressed in the introduction, my research is not prescriptive and ongoing mirror work is needed for ideological unlearning. While processing or reflecting on the implementation of practices, it's important to consider how we bring our whole self into pedagogical approaches. Creating an identity affirming space requires us to center humanity in our work. We consciously think about the alignment between our beliefs and actions, and co-construct learning spaces with students that honor their brilliance, histories, and identities.

DOI: 10.4324/9781003216964-5

Part II

3

Unpacking Identity

How are you going to get better as a human being, let alone an educator, if you are not willing to address your own beliefs and biases?

Val Brown (2017)

Prior to teaching, I thought I had the dynamics of the classroom environment all figured out. I purchased and saved children's books throughout the year of my student teaching, planned units of study, and bought décor to enhance the aesthetics of my future classroom. Following my first semester of student teaching, I received a letter of intent to work within a Reggio-inspired school for a kindergarten position. I could not wait to set up my classroom and personally reach out to students that summer before the start of school. In every practicum experience, professors talked about the power of relationships and the importance of knowing students to ignite learning. However, courses and discussions at the collegiate level did not delve deep into the complexities of identity, *how* one forms authentic connections, or the mirror work that is necessary to form an inclusive community.

We've all heard the saying, *"you don't know, what you don't know,"* yet as an educator committed to serving all children, there were things I should have known before working with youth and their families that first year of teaching. I should have known how to be responsive to the needs of deaf communities

DOI: 10.4324/9781003216964-6

and multilingual learners to form strong partnerships with students and their caregivers. I should have known how to address conversations about gender and sexual orientation when students questioned differences in familial structures. I should have been more aware of my text selections and content within assignments to avoid the projection of harmful stereotypes. In addition to unpacking academic standards, I should have also unpacked my understanding of diversity, identity, and how my social construction shaped instructional practices that needed to be disrupted.

We all hold multiple identities that influence how we see and interact with the world. The ways we view society and people is filtered through a lens of our cultural experiences. I went into teaching with the best intentions yet failed to understand how to validate the identities of all learners and their families. Texts displayed on bookshelves with images that looked like me were not enough. Signs or educational posters with the native languages of students were not enough. Inclusive statements or inspirational quotes on my walls were not enough. The work of building a cohesive, classroom community was not just about me getting my act together through self-work or the design of space, but also involved helping students to see each other as fully human.

What is Identity?

There are many theorists who have researched and published studies about identity development. Erik Erikson (1963) asserted that humans advance through eight stages in life hinged with conflict as a means to grow. Vander Zanden and Pace (1984), educational psychologists influenced by Erickson's theory, defined identity as one's placement within the world and an examination of self. Tajfel and Turner (1979) described identity as the way a person perceived themselves based their membership in social groups. The social identity theory (Tajfel & Turner, 1979) described how one's understanding of self connects to their interactions within the world; which continuously evolves over time and influences behaviors.

Janet Helms (1990) studied racial identity development and explained how it was a process that people of color navigated before white people while being exposed to racism in early stages of life. Through our experiences, we develop racial identity schemas that influence our actions (Helms & Cook, 1999). Racial identity development is the understanding of one's positionality in the context of race and internalized perspectives while existing in a racialized society. Helms developed the Racial Identity Social Interaction Model (RISIM), which "integrates concepts from the racial identity theory and power dynamics to describe racial dynamics that occur in group discussions about race" (Thrower, Helms, & Price, 2020, n.p.).

Kidd and Teagle (2012) referred to identity as the discernments and self-perceptions that are held by people in society. In other words, identity is formulated by how the individual sees themselves situated in the world. Through Kidd's research (2002), there are three forms of identity that consume our existence:

Individual identity—the humanity each person possesses in their own right.

Social identity—a sense of belonging to a group that reflects collectivism and shared experiences among members.

Cultural identity—connection to a distinct cultural or ethnic group.

Through the studies of theorists named and many unmentioned, we understand that identities are multifaceted and complex, reflecting not only how we see ourselves, but how others view us. When my sixth-grade teacher scolded white boys and yelled, "*Stop acting Black*," it became clear that my perception of my own racial identity was not vastly embraced by the world—*even by those who I thought loved me and had my back*. There are components to our identity that are socially constructed from our daily activities and the people who influence our lives. Additionally, there are identifiers that have been assigned to our personhood due to the biases, ignorance, and deficit ideologies that stem from the social development of others.

Kimberlé Crenshaw (1989), critical race theorist and legal scholar, coined the term intersectionality which describes how race, class, gender, and other parts of our identities are connected to inequitable systems that overlap. Through an intersectional lens, we see how forms of oppression function together and intensify based on social positions. Crenshaw wrote about intersectionality in the published paper "Demarginalizing the Intersection of Race and Sex" to emphasize how feminism and antiracist policies neglected the overlapping discrimination that Black women face. Patricia Hill Collins (2015) characterized intersectionality as an analysis of power where one studies how systems impact marginalized communities. If we can interrogate systems of power, we can begin to dream, dismantle, and heal from forms of oppression.

As a Black woman, my navigation in the world is significantly impacted by race. However, the injustices I experience are often exacerbated due to gender discrimination and the ableism I encounter in my everyday life while living with an invisible illness. I cannot begin to tell you how many times people inform me of what I could or should do, without taking my immunocompromised body into consideration or providing any accommodations. There are many intersections to our students' identities that we must be mindful of when developing systems that influence educational outcomes. The systems we create condition experiences and shape the stories students carry for a lifetime.

Students are constantly evaluating their place in the world and where they fit in social contexts. There are messages that permeate throughout society that signal who people should aspire to be and the identities that should be eschewed. It's hard to be free when you continuously feel the gaze from someone's binoculars into your life. There are youth who feel the need to tone down their authenticity or stand far from their truth while living up to someone else's expectations. As educators, we have the power to cultivate spaces that teach students to see *who they are and who they are not*. We can help students to see their lives as poetry in motion that exudes beauty and promise. However, it's a journey that involves us confronting biases, stereotypes, and deficit ideologies that strive to take away the love we have for ourselves and others.

Identity Threats

Deficit thinking and dehumanizing ideologies produce real identity threats and actions that hinder opportunities. Words that end in "ism" and "phobia" typically signal discriminatory behaviors that stem from harmful ideologies tied to one's social conditioning. These behaviors are learned and require a process of unlearning. We need to intentionally think about the beliefs we carry while working with students and help youth to think about the ideologies they bring into interpersonal relationships. There are many isms and phobias that could be named and unpacked, but here are a few to reference that have emerged often in my experiences of working with students and teachers:

◆ Ableism—discrimination or prejudice against people with disabilities (e.g., physical, intellectual, psychiatric, etc.).

◆ Antisemitism—discrimination, hostility, or prejudice against Jewish people.

◆ Classism—discrimination or hostility based on social class or economic status.

◆ Colorism— a product of racism where discrimination or prejudice is exhibited against people of color with darker skin tones within ethnic or racial groups.

◆ Fatophobia—discrimination, hostility, or prejudice against people with obesity.

◆ Homophobia—discrimination or hostility based on sexual orientation, prejudice against homosexuality.

◆ Islamophobia—discrimination, hostility, or prejudice against Muslims, practitioners of Islam.

◆ Racism—discrimination, hostility, or prejudice against people of color (revisit Chapter 1 for an in-depth definition with historical contexts)

◆ Transphobia—discrimination, hostility, or prejudice against people who identify as transgender

Imposter syndrome, stereotype threat, the model minority myth, and binary thinking also impact the ways we see ourselves and others. Imposter syndrome is the internal belief that one is unworthy of recognition, accomplishments, and the credibility others may see in them. Psychologists Pauline Rose Clance and Suzzana Imes (1978) initially described the imposter phenomenon in the context of high-achieving women. The research was not intersectional nor took historical or sociopolitical contexts and the impact of white supremacy culture into consideration (Burey & Tulshyan, 2021). In Dena Simmons' national TedTalk (2016), *How Students of Color Confront Imposter Syndrome*, she conveyed how some youth of color may attach feelings of fraudulence to their achievements while navigating in spaces with a stronghold of whiteness that produce the feeling of being othered. These feelings are not the fault of the student, but the fault of the systems adults create.

Stereotype threat may also impact the performance and experiences of students across race and gender. Claude Steele and Joshua Aronson (1995) define stereotype threat as "the risk of confirming, as self-characteristic, a negative stereotype about one's group" (p. 797). I have worked with students who have refrained from being authentic to avoid being seen as a threat or problematic due to internalized stereotypes about their own racial or gender identity. Youth also adopt stereotypical beliefs about race due to racial disparities that are visible in school environments (e.g., disciplinary referrals, lack of racial representation in high ability or honors programming, etc.). I was invited to listen to high school students present research projects at Hamilton Southeastern High School related to environmental and school inequities. One group of students specifically addressed action research pertaining to the lack of racial representation in advanced placement courses. A white, female student started the presentation by sharing how her counselors and teachers highly encouraged her to consider courses that were not on her radar. She disclosed to an audience that included administrators and school board members how she entered the action research project with the belief that students of color did not want to take advantage of rigorous courses and assumed that outreach for enrollment and encouragement were the same for all students. Through collaboration and cross-cultural dialogues with students of color in her group, she learned and conveyed to the audience that many of her peers from minoritized groups were not afforded the same *"you should consider this"* talk from adults, and in some cases, were discouraged despite their desires due to counselors who deemed that the workload would be unmanageable. What stereotypes were absorbed about race that would lead adults to encourage the participation of white students and dissuade students of color from enrolling in AP courses due to workload? How many other students carry stereotypes due to observable disparities and the conditions of school environments?

The model minority myth is the perception that certain marginalized communities are apt to prosper and experience success at a higher degree than other minoritized groups (Lee, 2009). This stereotypical belief of innate talent or aptitude for achievement is often applied to Asian Americans—*and let's be clear, this myth despite positive implications is damaging*. Sarah Soon-Ling Blackburn (2019) described in the Learning for Justice article, "What is the Model Minority Myth?" how typecasts exclude differences with racial and ethnic groups and dismiss the racism Asian Americans encounter in their lived experiences. She explained how school systems may fail to meet the diverse needs of students (particularly Asian American youth who struggle academically) when teachers adhere to the myth, casting Asian communities as a monolithic group. This myth is also harmful to Asian Americans who internalize it and feel pressured to uphold socially constructed expectations.

From the Chinese Exclusion Act in 1882 to Japanese internment camps, there has been a long-standing history of racism and misogyny that has harmed Asian American and Pacific Islander (AAPI) groups. Due to the rhetoric used to describe COVID-19 under the Trump administration, xenophobia, and racism, there has been a rise in violence against Asian American communities including a mass shooting in Atlanta, Georgia in 2021. From March 2020 to December 2020, there were 2,800 anti-Asian American hate incidents, according to the online self-reporting tool, called Stop AAPI Hate (2021). When people uphold the model minority myth and cast Asian Americans as a billboard image of the American Dream it disregards the racism many face and continue to experience.

Binary thinking is another identity threat that influences how we see people, particularly gender. The terms *sex and gender* are often used interchangeably despite having distinct meanings. Gender refers to a person's understanding of themself as a gendered being (Price & Skolnik, 2017). It is situated on a continuum that does not limit one to exist as either a male or a female (e.g., intersex which refers to individuals who are born with any of several variations in sex characteristics including chromosomes, sex hormones or genitals, etc.). Gender expression refers to the behaviors tied to the social construction of gender identity, incorporating the micro-decisions made from physical appearance to forms of communication. The biological attributes of an individual is known as one's sex. When the biological attributes correspond to a person's gender identity, one is described as cisgender (Mayo, 2014; Price & Skolnik, 2017). A person who identifies as transgender does not feel an alignment between their gender identity and sex assigned at birth. For example, a person may be born with the biological anatomy of a male, thus assigned male at birth, yet their gender identity aligns with socially constructed roles and expressions of a female—in this case, identifying as a transgender woman. There are also individuals who do not conform to the confines of any gender identity, identifying as non-binary.

When we view the world through a binary lens, we erase the gender diverse experiences our students may bring into the classroom environment. As early as the age of two (Stennes, Burch, Sen, & Bauer, 2005), children are aware of gender identity, oftentimes because they are socialized into these understandings long before they are born. From the pinks and blues of gender reveals (which is really identifying sex) to the gifts received from baby showers, many children are exposed early on to binary thinking. I have worked with numerous students from primary to secondary grades, who identify as transgender or non-binary, championing gender-inclusive policies and practices. As a preservice teacher, I did not receive any formal education or pre-service teaching course that would have equipped me to think about gender inclusivity in the classroom environment. Yet, I was committed to self-work and unlearning. I was committed to building authentic connections with youth and their families. I was committed to becoming a better human. And when you're committed, you do the work.

There are many other identity threats outside what has been highlighted, which reflected personal experiences or circumstances that involved partnerships and collaborative problem-solving with teachers, students, and caregivers. I alluded to the ableism I experience in my own life and know discriminatory practices against students with disabilities are a real threat. Patriarchy, misogyny, xenophobia, tokenism, sexism, and more are harmful to humanity. The Combahee River Collective (1977) of Black feminists reminds us to think about the interlocking ways race, gender, and sexuality influence our navigation, but emphasize how racism is a thread that impacts all identities. In *LGBTQ Youth and Education: Policies and Practices* (2014), Cris Mayo stated:

> LGBTQ communities are often structured by white dominance and are unwilling to see how whiteness structures ideas about who is legitimately LGBTQ or who can easily access LGBTQ community resources and social spaces. This white dominance may be expressed through overt racism or implicitly assume what gayness means and thus be unwilling to recognize the sexual and gender identities that emerge within racial and ethnic communities.
>
> (p. 27)

All forms of oppression are connected and if we address the pervasiveness of racism, we have the ability to positively impact all communities.

The following will discuss how to address identity threats in the classroom, including considerations for gender-inclusive environments.

Dismantling Identity Threats

An identity affirming environment embraces the full humanity of students, and educators work to eliminate the threats that impact one's sense of belonging and educational experience. We know that stress manifests in people differently and draws different responses. When our bodies experience chronic stress from an environment, the function of the brain is significantly impacted in ways that are detrimental to learning. Stress can harm the hippocampus, where we convert moments of life into long-term memories (Goleman, 2012). Cortisol, the primary stress hormone, contributes to the disconnection of neural pathways that affect our ability to think and process information. Identity threats not only influence how students feel about themselves and others, but ultimately affect their physical health and learning—*and that goes for us as adults too!* If we want our students to thrive, it's critical to eliminate the identity threats.

Identity Work

Val Brown, equity advocate and scholar, stated in a Center for Teaching Quality article (2017), that "we [educators] as a profession, have to stop trying to avoid doing the work of dealing with implicit bias and racism within our midst" and reminds us to embrace the work of addressing our biases and beliefs to become better humans. To form connections with others, we must first have a sense of self. This involves opportunities that enhance identity development and affirm the histories students bring into the classroom. There are powerful tools in the universe, such as Learning for Justice's anti-bias framework that incorporates identity standards (K-12) and activities, such as "I Am From" poems (Ahmed, 2018) that can help students think about their positioning in the world. Each educational experience, unit of study, or lesson can serve as an invitation for students to learn more about themselves, including strengths and empathy for others. When planning instructional practices and reviewing content, we can ask ourselves the following essential questions to integrate identity work in curriculum:

- What aspects of my lesson or unit of study promote self-love and reflect a mirror that affirms the identities of learners?
- How am I providing space for students to express their individuality and authenticity?
- How am I helping students to see their strengths, intellectual capabilities, and build self-confidence through the implementation of instruction?
- How am I creating a brave space for students to use their voice and understand its power?

To change the vision of teaching and learning within an institution, you can elevate these reflective points in curriculum spaces and advocate for their use as essential questions in planning for instructional lessons. We reach students in profound ways when we humanize content, center their identities, and honor their voice in instructional settings and curriculum. The reflective questions help us to center students in the creation of work that supports their learning.

Identify and Monitor Biases

Teaching students about the brain and how thoughts are formulated through a lens of culture can help students understand how biases are developed. Every day we see and hear new information that we compartmentalize and utilize when trying to make meaning of phenomena around us. We can explain to students how our brain makes associations and connects attributes to people based on what we've internalized through experiences. Everyone harbors biases and those functions of our mind do not always lead to negative outcomes. Biases can be a mechanism of our survival, yet we must be watchful of how they influence our interactions with others. If we want students to learn about biases to mitigate threats, it's critical to teach concepts of neuroscience research. Students need to understand how to identify and monitor biases that derive from their social construction.

Teach neuroscience: Explain to students how the brain creates patterns and associations. An introductory exercise for anti-bias education could include a mini-lesson where students of all ages receive a list of words (e.g., *peanut butter, McDonald's, beach, rain, etc.*) and are tasked to name the first thing they think about after reading each term. The exercise demonstrates the automaticity of our associations. Our brain is wired for making connections. For instance, when I see the word *McDonald's* I don't even have to think twice before the thought of a Happy Meal comes to mind (as the parent of a child who couldn't care less about the food but wants the "surprise" toy). When we are aware of the cognitive shorthands our brain formulates, then we can be more mindful of how we make decisions and see each other. Constant exposure to particular viewpoints and people conditions our navigation, and we have to teach students how the brain influences operations.

Teach how to identify biases: Point out stereotypical and biased views in the moment. Literature, media and films, articles, and other curricular materials are full of biases that could be used as examples and teachable moments while working with students. Question the attributes and interests assigned to literary characters. What messages are being sent when characters or people are portrayed in stereotypical ways (e.g., the domestication of women, poverty in communities of color, etc.)? Teach students how to identify biased sources, informing the difference between one's opinion and factual information. Many state standards require students to draw inferences from text and analyze literary themes, which can encapsulate learning about biases.

Teach how to monitor biases: Through explicit teaching we can help students identify biases in instructional materials and different contexts. When students are able to name what is biased, they can process that information and determine how it will guide their decisions or interactions with others moving forward. We can create a space for these conversations by asking students what they are noticing and inquiring how they will apply their learning in social situations.

Developing time for conversations and dialogues about bias—*whether in a morning meeting, whole group instructional setting, or student conference*—helps with identity development. Through knowing ourselves we can begin to understand how we show up for others.

Build Empathy

When you step outside of yourself and experience the emotions (e.g., pain, grief, etc.) of another person, you're practicing empathy (Ioannidou & Konstantikaki, 2008). The identity threats students face within school environments often reflect spaces where empathy has not been cultivated. Empathy promotes collectivism and a sense of belonging. It's a precursor to building trust and partnerships. Students need time to collaborate and learn from each other, and we can explicitly teach students how to engage in mindful communication, whether verbal or non-verbal. When we commit to active listening or seek to understand, we think about the ways we arrive into a conversation and read the body language within the room. Conversation stems can be helpful for students of all ages to practice empathy and provide a reflective pause for processing different perspectives.

Could you explain what you meant by …
Based on what you shared, I understand …
How can I help?
Help me understand what upset you …
What do you need for support?

Conversation stems support communication that yields empathy and understanding. There are many benefits to learning about responsive forms of communication. Students will effectively handle conflict if they deem a challenging situation as a teachable moment or opportunity for learning through active listening. Conversation protocols during whole-group instruction also condition a culture of engagement. When students are in a space where a dialogue is taking place, they can implement the use of sentence starters that build off the thoughts and deliberations of peers.

I affirm what you are saying, it reminds me of a time when …

Thank you for sharing. I also agree with …

I listened to your perspective and disagreed with … because …

Early childhood educators can incorporate similar strategies to generate an environment that honors voice. Young learners are capable of having conversations that foster affirmations, connections, and empathy. As a former kindergarten teacher, students practiced the following:

Thank you for sharing. I really liked when you said …

Your story reminded me of a time when …

When you talked about …, I felt … because …

Students should not feel limited to respond in the framing of the protocols or conversation stems, but the strategies are certainly a way to elicit mindful communication. You can also self-evaluate your own class and gauge the climate of your culture. *Do I have a classroom that reflects a culture of empathy?* The self-assessment shown in Figure 3.1 can demonstrate strengths and opportunities for growth.

When reviewing your self-reflection, you can also think about students who need support in different areas; furthermore, analyzing the trends or patterns documented. *What hinders the building of empathy? Do students feel safe to speak authentically or have a sense of belonging that eases engagement with peers?* Building empathy among students is a process, and in human work, we should never lose sight of our own emotions and how our feelings guide interactions.

Disrupt Harmful Ideologies

> The core of identity threats is an ideology that someone carries about humanity into experiences.

As humans, we tend to see the world through our lived experiences. We are all socially conditioned to see situations in particular ways and the ideologies we possess influence how we filter knowledge in our brains.

Culture of empathy	Often	Sometimes	Never	Evidence
Students actively listen to each other in various contexts (e.g., whole group, paired collaboration, etc.)·				
Students make connections to the expressions and thoughts of peers.				
Students offer affirmations within discussions to honor voices and perspectives of peers.				
Students seek to understand.				
Students approach conflict as a teachable moment and ask for clarity.				
Students are conscious of the emotions and feelings of peers.				

FIGURE 3.1 Culture of Empathy

Our avoidance of identity threats will not make them go away. And we cannot use hope as a strategy, *hoping* inequities and interpersonal relationships between students will work themselves out. *When we see discriminatory acts against people with disabilities, we must disrupt it. When we hear dehumanizing language, we must disrupt it. When we see sexist behaviors, we must disrupt it.* We must disrupt acts in the moment, and then address the ideology that evoked the response.

When the harm is disrupted, we start the healing process on an individual and collective level. Talk to the student who caused harm and question the beliefs that led to the action. Oftentimes, there's a tendency to swiftly handle a situation by telling a student what was wrong and how they won't do it again. However, the swiftness can be a missed opportunity to debrief and unpack ideologies. *What made you believe it was appropriate to address your peer in this way? Help me understand where that belief or thinking came from?* Notice, I'm not using the infamous question, *"Why did you do this?"* to only get an *"I was mad"* response. We need to identify the harmful ideologies and help students to reconstruct their thinking (Donatelli-Bow, personal interview, 2021).

Repair Harm

Once the harm has been identified and ideologies have been unpacked, it's important to teach students why the behavior was problematic and think through alternative approaches in the context of similar situations. As mentioned, healing needs to happen on an individual and collective level. Therefore, the student who caused the harm will need to take ownership in the process of repairing the community. Through restorative practices (see Chapter 5), the student learns how to restore and repair the harm that affected others.

Here are some perspectives from students and teachers on eliminating identity threats and creating a welcoming environment:

> The most powerful way to eliminate identity threats in the classroom will always come back to relationships. Students know when a teacher knows their name, values getting to know them, and cares about them just as they are. As a music teacher, I have the amazing opportunity of having every single student in the entire school and I work hard to make sure it is apparent that my room is a safe space where students can come and be themselves. I think sometimes students need to hear you verbalize that out loud. "My room values all people, and you can always come to me if there is something I can do to help you because you deserve to be treated with respect." It's important that a teacher immediately shuts down any comments or behavior from others that would threaten someone's identity. Educators can set the tone for their classroom environment and I have sadly seen some classrooms where it is evident that a culture has been created where students think it is acceptable to say harmful things to others. In my classroom, I try to make sure students can see

themselves in our lessons, songs, videos, and classroom walls. Music naturally creates a space where conversations about identity, humanity, and empathy are constantly weaved throughout all we do.

(Lisa Finn, middle school music teacher)

In some of my classes, it is obvious that teachers are affirming because they have signs and posters in their room. Another way that I know if teachers are affirming is by what they teach in their curriculum. One day I was talking to my friends about how specific teachers treat students and how some teachers are good at making students feel welcome in their classroom. One of my friends said that they really like it when a teacher asks for their pronouns. I think this is a good way for teachers to show students that they care about them and respect them. I think that if teachers put in the effort to make students feel welcome and respected, then there could be a better school environment for all students.

(Teagan Chandler, junior)

Teachers can have a welcome mat out when I enter the classroom. They can greet me by saying good morning and giving me a hug. They can also use a polite and calm tone, not mean. Another thing they can do is use kind and helpful words while teaching others how to be nice.

(Jaelynne Rent, third grade)

Every student will have a unique, different take on what they need to feel a part of a community. Therefore, it is best to intentionally ask students what is necessary to help them feel seen and heard rather than making assumptions. The accounts from students (i.e., Teagan and Jaelynne) highlight *spaces for connectivity, equity-minded educators, inclusive language, and the design of the classroom* as important factors for a welcoming environment. The next chapter will delve deeper into aspects of the physical classroom environment and demonstrate questions that can be used to gather insightful feedback from students. There is much we can learn from youth if we provide opportunities for them to amplify their voice.

Students who are a part of the LGBTQ+ community are vulnerable to discriminatory practices when environments are shaped with binary thinking about gender identity and sexual orientation. When equity is at the forefront of our praxis, we construct classrooms and school cultures that center the identities of students and understand the factors that can interfere with inclusivity. Through my work in DEI spaces, I have conducted many gender diversity trainings with co-conspirator Morgan Donatelli-Bow, who is a fierce advocate and member of the LGBTQ+ community. Donatelli-Bow is the founder of the LGBTQ+ working group of Indiana's Protection for Abused and Trafficked Humans Task Force. She offers the following considerations for creating a gender-inclusive environment:

◆ *Literature.* Every child deserves to see themselves represented in literature. Whether it is in the classroom or the school library, books representing LGBTQ+ families or talking about gender identity and diversity should be readily available to all students.

◆ *Inclusive language.* The ways we communicate with our students often, and sometimes unintentionally, reinforce gender dichotomies. Instead of using gendered language and saying, "Good morning, boys and girls" you can say "Good morning, everyone." In primary grades, instead of lining up students by gender, assemble them up based on interests or just allow them to line up with no parameters.

◆ *Respecting names and pronouns.* LGBTQ+ students should be able to be their authentic selves in the classroom. Students, as early as primary grades, may request to go by different pronouns or ask to go by a gender-neutral name based on revelations of their own identity and how they choose to identify. As educators, respecting students' pronouns and names is a great way to make students feel safe in your classroom.

- *Inclusive signage.* If a student feels safe in the classroom, they are in a better position to take in the information that is being taught to them. Inclusive signage is a way to help LGBTQ+ students feel safe. This can be done through a sign in the classroom that reads "All are welcome here" or even a Safe Space sticker in the window. Importantly, affirming features in a classroom environment must be coupled with anti-bias, inclusive actions.

- *LGBTQ+ representation in your curriculum.* From math and science to English and history, members of the LGBTQ+ community have contributed to every major subject taught in school. Include important figures from your subject areas in your lessons and normalize the fact that a member of the LGBTQ+ community has a place in history.

- *Affinity spaces* (see Chapter 6). LGBTQ+ youth need spaces that are inclusive of their shared lived experiences. The presence of a Gender Sexuality Alliance (GSA) not only promotes an affinity space for LGBTQ+ youth but has also been found to reduce bullying and suicidal ideation. According to the 2016 research study of the University of California Berkeley with approximately 63,000 participants, "LGBTQ students at schools with GSAs were 36% less likely to be fearful for their own safety." GSAs or affinity spaces for LGBTQ+ youth also serve "as vehicles for social change related to racial, gender and educational justice".

(Aspegren, 2020)

 **Mirror Work**

Many of us have experienced *when keeping it real goes wrong moments.* Think about a time when you entered a challenging conversation about a humanity-related topic that may have spiraled and generated strong emotions. What ideologies did you bring into the conversation in comparison to the other person?

Where did those ideologies come from? If you had more time to process, would you have entered that conversation differently?

Say Their Names

Names hold value and meaning to people (Ahmed, 2018). They provide a sense of individuality and affirmation when used in social contexts. Students should be called by their names and what makes them feel authentic. Cooper, Haney, Krieg and Brownell (2017) conducted a study that examined the use of names in biology courses where more than 85% of 157 students conveyed that it was important for instructors to know their name. As educators, we cannot be dismissive of the power of names and resort to sobriquets when we struggle to pronounce them. An identity-affirming space honors the names of students. As culturally responsive educators, we should practice saying names until we get them right. If you utilize the **Systems Work** framework (see Chapter 2) and identify student recognition as a school-wide inequity, you can collectively work with colleagues and develop structures to ensure that names are accurately pronounced. Here's an example of how one teacher librarian, JoyAnn Boudreau, worked to assemble a team to address the mispronunciation of student names through a systematic approach:

> My school, located in Central Indiana, has an Equity Team of two coaches and typically around a dozen total members. Some of our best conversations are planned and on the agenda, but sometimes great work can be done from a topic raised spontaneously that our educators are seeing around the school. A teacher came into a meeting one day a couple of years ago understandably agitated that her child, a student in the building, had a guest (substitute) teacher who caused her child to feel othered and judged for her name remarking, "No, you can't be 'X.' This is a boy's name. What is YOUR name?" This led us to conversations about hearing others in school make remarks such as, "I have no idea how to say your name," "I'm never going to

be able to say that," and how students who are not white are more likely to experience these microaggressions.

Everyone on the team passionately agreed that names are important and a part of how we build relationships with students to make them feel seen. A suggestion was made to create name pronunciation keys for guest teachers school wide. Some of our teachers already were implementing this practice, but we saw a need to have it be systematic. We discussed the need to annotate pronunciations [make notes on the pronunciations of names] for all students, so that teachers are not othering names they feel personally are different or difficult. Additionally, not all teachers or guest teachers may need assistance with the same names, so we needed to do this for all names. We also thought this could be a teachable moment for students to talk about the value of names and self-advocacy.

Clear Vision of Diversity, Equity, and Inclusion (DEI) Work

We know that the mission and aspirational goals of a school can influence the work that occurs within the classroom environment. There may be building-level teams in place to address school improvement plans (SIP), yet everyone has a role in making an environment more inclusive and equitable. Considering the national controversy where predominantly white communities and state legislators are pushing against any form of identity work in schools (i.e., SEL), I think it's important to be clear about what DEI work is and what it is not. First, let's talk about diversity. What does diversity mean to your organization? No, for *real*, what does it really mean? From headlines where books are banned due to content featuring homosexuality to Black students being forced to cut their hair to be a part of an organization, we need to be clear on what diversity really means.

Diversity is a representation of differences. It reflects who is in the room, while inclusion speaks to how we create a sense of belonging. *How do we make people within the room feel as if they matter? In what ways do we value everyone's identity and strengths?* Equity is ensuring that people within the room have what they need to thrive. It requires us to acknowledge the barriers that students face, with a keen eye on marginalized groups to make sure that schools are providing equitable access and opportunities to all students. We also need to think about the levels of support that are provided to families that foster partnerships. There should be congruence between the ways we care for students and their caregivers.

Research shows that when students feel psychologically safe, they are able to learn. When students are confronted with identity threats such as racism, sexism, classism, or homophobia, it impacts their emotional health and well-being. Neuroscience research demonstrates that we as human beings are wired for connection. This is human work. It's about the way we see and respond to people. For educators, if we're going to create an optimal learning environment for students, we must be aware of our own biases and make an intentional effort to teach our students how to respect and see each other as fully human. It's about cultivating spaces where students understand the importance of empathy, and teaching students how to communicate and collaborate with each other. This is only one of the many aspects of DEI work.

DEI work also entails understanding how students learn best so educators can respond to their instructional needs. It requires educators to be culturally responsive, where we build learning partnerships with students. Building a partnership means we know who we are serving, including the families or caregivers of students. Therefore, it's important for educators to be knowledgeable of racially, culturally, and linguistically diverse backgrounds, and understand the abilities of students to create spaces that are compatible with their learning. It's not indoctrination nor divisive to teach students how to care for humanity and support their individualized needs. The ideologies people bring and their lack of understanding the work is the problem, which is why schools need to have a clear vision of equity that is commonly understood by all staff.

Deepening Understandings of Identity in the Classroom

It is important for all students to have a positive sense of self and come to an understanding of their identity as a learner and contributing member of the world. If we want students to see themselves as readers, writers, and mathematicians, then the conditions for learning should reflect opportunities that invite students into those roles. Identity work can be implemented across all content areas. When I work with schools, I typically hear how discussions about humanity are more fitting for language arts, history, science (e.g., theories, etc.), arts, and physical education courses that center health inequities. However, there are many educators who struggle to see how this work can take shape in mathematics and other content areas.

In mathematics courses, sociopolitical contexts can be explored in quantitative ways. Students can explore real-world experiences that involve a critical analysis of social inequities (Buchanan-Rivera, 2021), which could include learning about gender wage gaps to the examinations of historical redlining. My primary grade students had math journals that incorporated inquiries reflective of lived experiences that prompted deeper conversations about humanity. For instance, a math problem asking students to calculate items bought in a grocery store could have led to a deeper discussion about access, food deserts, and social advocacy. The humanization of mathematics is important for students to connect mathematical thinking to culture, language, and their everyday lives (Dingle & Yeh, 2021).

The sustainability of society is contingent upon human connections. Young children need exposure to people who do not mirror their image of self. As emphasized, literature paired with anti-bias work is a vehicle for students to see a world beyond familiarized contexts. We can also think about the voices centered in curricular experiences, making careful considerations when inviting guests, planning field visits, and using other forms of media (e.g., documentary, films, etc.). As students become older and understand fairness or justice, they can begin to reflect on their positionality in the world (see Chapter 5) and think critically about the messages school environments send. There are many ways for students to express themselves and whether through writing prompts or wellness conferences where you check on the well-being of students, you can have them highlight one of these reflections of human work:

H   How does the classroom environment **honor humanity**?
U   How does my teacher demonstrate an **understanding** of my intellectual and/or emotional needs?
M   Which learning experiences in the classroom are **memorable**, leaving a lasting impression?
A   How does the classroom **affirm** my identity?
N   What happens in school or the classroom that may **negate** values of equity and inclusion?

Feedback should elevate our praxis and inform us of areas of growth. Yet, we must be vulnerable and open to seeing ourselves through the eyes of students. There's power in listening to students and allowing their voice to be a guide in decisions that advance equity. Every lesson constructed and systems developed should be crafted for the benefit of students. We need to remember the human aspect of this work.

Cultural autobiographies are also a powerful component of identity work that can help older students have an in-depth understanding of self. We have all adopted norms, values, and perspectives that derive from our social contexts and upbringings. The self-work of knowing our identity is a personal journey where reflections about race, cross-cultural relationships, religion, class, and many other experiences can be explored. Here is framing I have used for cultural autobiographies that could be used as a part of students' writing journals, humanities courses, and other literary experiences:

Understanding Identity

How do you identify yourself?
Who has influenced your aspirations of self?
How do families, caregivers, the geographical location of our upbringings, and other relevant parts to the formation of self, develop personal value systems?

Understanding Others

How were you taught to value differences?
How have your social experiences in the world influenced the way you see people who do not share your identity?

Understanding Navigation

What has been learned through your understanding of self?
What things will you consider with a renewed understanding of self as you interact and respond to others?

While working at the collegiate level as an adjunct professor, my students would often share how they wished more K-12 teachers would have engaged in identity work. There are adults who believe children should be guarded from conversations about race, identity, and the injustices in the world. However, there is a detriment to shielding students from conversations and cultural understandings that are a critical part of human development. The violence, hate, and prejudice that often dims the light in the world reflect deficits in ideologies and teachings about humanity. We owe our students truth and spaces of love where they can learn to find the beauty within themselves and others.

Chapter Highlights

- ◆ We all have multiple identities that influence how we see humanity, interact with people, and navigate systems in society.
- ◆ Many identity threats exist that we need to identify and dismantle in efforts to create an affirming environment.
- ◆ It is important for students to understand how their brain works and the formulation of biases that hinder us from seeing people as fully human.
- ◆ School leaders and educators need a clear understanding of DEI work, and a strong vision for developing spaces of belonging. This is human work.
- ◆ The classroom is a space for identity and human development, including brave conversations about humanity.

 **Collective Work**

Create a brave space within a staff meeting or grade level planning session to think about your own cultural autobiographies. You can determine protocols for a vulnerable conversation with *willing* participants. I would not force anyone to share, as someone's story is not owed to anyone. However, I emphasize that adults need to practice having critical conversations before engaging in discussions with students. Our delivery and the consciousness we bring into critical conversations make a difference in the experiences students have in the classroom—*there are lots of educational horror stories out there about teachers who entered discussions ill-prepared.* In addition to the reflective questions in the **Understanding Navigation** section, think about how your narrative influences teaching and learning, and the systems that exist within your classroom.

References

Ahmed, S. (2018). *Being the Change: Lessons and Strategies to Teach Social Comprehension*. Portsmouth, NH: Heinemann.

Aspegren, Elinor. (2020, June 15). Want to tackle LGBTQ bullying at your middle or high school? Start a gay-straight alliance, study says. *USA Today.* www.usatoday.com/story/news/nation/2020/06/15/lgbtq-bullying-gay-straight-alliance-schools-study/5346463002/

Blackburn, S. (2019, March 21). What is the Model Minority Myth? *Learning for Justice.* www.learningforjustice.org/magazine/what-is-the-model-minority-myth

Brown, V. (2017, October 19). Hiring Black teachers only solves part of the problem. *CTQ.* www.teachingquality.org/hiring-black-teachers-only-solves-part-of-the-problem/

Buchanan-Rivera, E. (2021). Courageous Community Conversations. *Indiana Mathematics Teacher.*

Burey, J. & Tulshyan, R. (2021, February 11). *Stop Telling Women they have Imposter Syndrome.* https://hbr.org/2021/02/stop-telling-women-they-have-imposter-syndrome

Clance, P.R., & Imes, S.A. (1978). The imposter phenomenon in high achieving women: Dynamics and therapeutic intervention. *Psychotherapy: Theory, Research & Practice, 15*(3), 241. DOI: 10.1037/h0086006

Collins, P. (2015). Intersectionality's definition dilemmas. *Annual Review of Sociology.* DOI: 10.1146/annurev-soc-073014-112142

Combahee River Collective (1977). *The Combahee River Collective Statement.* www.blackpast.org/african-american-history/combahee-river-collective-statement-1977/

Cooper, K.M., Haney, B., Krieg, A., & Brownell, S.E. (2017). What's in a name? The importance of students perceiving that an instructor knows their names in a high-enrollment biology classroom. *Cell Biology Education—Life Sciences Education, 16*(Spring), 1–13.

Crenshaw, K. (1989). Demarginalizing the intersection of race and sex: A Black feminist critique of antidiscrimination doctrine, feminist theory and antiracist politics. *University of Chicago Legal Forum, 1*(8).http://chicagounbound.uchicago.edu/uclf/vol1989/iss1/8

Dingle, M., & Yeh, C. (2021). Mathematics in context: The pedagogy of liberation. *Learning for Justice.* www.learningforjustice.org/magazine/spring-2021/mathematics-in-context-the-pedagogy-of-liberation

Erikson, E. (1963). *Childhood and Society.* New York NY: Macmillan.

Goleman, D. (2012). The sweet spot for achievement. *Psychology Today.* www.psychologytoday.com/us/blog/the-brain-and-emotional-intelligence/201203/the-sweet-spot-achievement

Helms, J. (Ed.). (1990). *Black and White Racial Identity: Theory, Research, and Practices.* Santa Barbara, CA: Greenwood Press.

Helms, J.E., & Cook, Donelda. (1999). *Using Race and Culture in Counseling and Psychotherapy: Theory and Process.* Boston, MA: Allyn & Bacon.

Ioannidou, F., & Konstantikaki, V. (2008, September–December). Empathy and emotional intelligence: What is it really about? *International Journal of Caring Sciences, 1*(3), 118–123.

Kidd, Warren (2002). *Culture and Identity* (1st ed.). New York, NY: Palgrave Macmillan.

Kidd, Warren, & Teagle, Alison. (2012). *Culture and Identity* (2nd ed.). New York, NY: Palgrave Macmillan.

Lee, S.J. (2009). *Unraveling the Model Minority Stereotype: Listening to Asian American Youth* (2nd ed.). New York, NY: Teachers College Press.

Mayo, C. (2014). *LGBTQ Youth and Education: Policies and Practices.* New York, NY: Teachers College Press.

Price, M., & Skolnik, A. (2017). *The Sage Encyclopedia of Psychology and Gender.* Thousand Oaks, CA: Sage.

Simmons, D. (2016, December 15). How students of color confront impostor syndrome. *TED Talks.* www.ted.com/talks/dena_simmons_how_students_of_color_confront_impostor_syndrome?language=en

Steele, C.M., & Aronson, J. (1995). Stereotype threat and the intellectual test performance of African Americans. *Journal of Personality and Social Psychology, 69*(5), 797–811. doi:10.1037/0022-3514.69.5.797

Stennes, L.M., Burch, M.M., Sen, M.G., & Bauer, P.J. (2005). A longitudinal study of gendered vocabulary and communicative action in young children. *Developmental Psychology, 41,* 75–88.

Stop AAPI Hate. (2021, March 16). 2020–2021 national report. https://stopaapihate.org/2020-2021-national-report/

Tajfel, H., & Turner, J.C. (1979). An integrative theory of intergroup conflict. In W.G. Austin & S. Worchel (Eds.), *The Social Psychology of Intergroup Relations* (pp. 33–47). Monterey, CA: Brooks-Cole.

Thrower, S.J., Helms, J.E., & Price, M. (2020). Racial dynamics in counselor training: The racial identity social interaction model. *The Journal of Counselor Preparation and Supervision, 13*(1). doi:10.7729/131.1313

Vander Zanden, J., & Pace, A. (1984). *Educational Psychology: In Theory and Practice* (2nd ed.). New York, NY: Random House.

4

Intentional Spaces of Belonging

If students are to see themselves as intellectual beings, they must step into schools and classrooms where intellectualism is deeply seeded, expected, and nurtured.

Gholdy Muhammad (2020, p. 108)

The Language of Space

Let's close our eyes, breathe deeply, and imagine.

You walk into a room with leveled rows of cushioned seats. While standing you observe your surroundings. There are cup holders strategically designed in the center of each armchair. The beams from a projector portray an image onto a large screen. Each chair is aligned to face the depictions. The lights begin to dim, and background music emerges. How will you respond?

At a work-related event, you find yourself in an open room with a variety of tables. As you walk throughout the space, servers generously distribute a variety of hors d'oeuvres. Since you would prefer to sit down while devouring food, you find an open seat at a nearby table. You continue to indulge in the item foreign to your taste buds and notice that two other individuals have joined your table. While sitting at the table, you make eye contact with the people next to you. Based on your proximity to individuals and location, what is your next move?

DOI: 10.4324/9781003216964-7

You're running late to an appointment. As you walk into the designated building, you swiftly turn to your right and enter an elevator. After a few flights and an unsettling experience when the doors do not open immediately, you arrive at your destination. Upon entering the room, you notice a variety of seats in a scatter formation. Magazines reside next to the chairs. Additionally, a couple of televisions are positioned in different corners of the room. After registering with the receptionist, you look around the environment. What will you decide to do?

Our bodies are conditioned to respond to environmental stimuli. In a movie theater, we are inclined to sit in a comfortable seat, place our Sprite or preferred drink in the cup holder, and focus our attention on the screen. The dim lighting signals for the minimization of voice levels. We are wired to comply with the expectations of the theater space based on how it is designed. It would be unconventional if every participant stood up and looked in a direction away from the display. The size of the screen indicates a focal point, and the seats determine how we should be positioned. Table arrangements elicit social interaction. We will more than likely engage in a conversation while sitting at a table with people, as opposed to an arrangement of isolated chairs. And as for the waiting room, the layout and materials train our bodies to pause before an anticipated event.

We can intentionally design spaces to have a distinct purpose. The objects, layout, lighting, and structures within a space shape our response. Students spend a significant amount of time in educational environments (Jackson, 1990). They internalize the overt and hidden messages generated from their surroundings. Classroom environments not only mold our operations, but also transmit messages about our values and beliefs about learners.

> We can make our image of children and their capabilities visible through the human-centered spaces we create.

Design of Space

The spatial structure of a classroom refers to the seating arrangement of students, how a space fosters mobility, the proximity between students and teachers, and the climate of the instructional setting (Savage, 1999). As custodians of environments, we should consider how the layout and design of space contributes to identity development and the emotional well-being of students. Classroom environments must reflect a balance of individualistic and collectivist spaces. Students should have a space to work independently where they can construct their own knowledge and reflect on their identity as a learner. We also know that our identities are shaped through our social construction and the interactions we have with others. The seating and furniture arrangements of classrooms can foster social experiences, relationships, and ways students engage in learning.

Trumbull and a team of researchers developed the Bridging Cultures Project within selected Southern California schools to foster learning partnerships and implement a practical framework that integrated cultural differences in the design of classroom organization and management (Trumbull, Rothstein-Fisch, Greenfield, & Quiroz, 2001). The intent of the project was to make environments culturally responsive and conducive for learning (Rothstein-Fisch & Trumbull, 2008). "In the majority of the Bridging Cultures classrooms, students were from immigrant Latino populations" (Rothstein-Fisch & Trumbull, 2008, p. xviii). Each teacher within the study learned value systems of individualism and collectivism as a framework for responsive teaching. The team of researchers observed, interviewed, and recorded the efforts of teachers implementing the framework over the course of five years (Trumbull, Rothstein-Fisch, Greenfield, & Quiroz, 2001).

Some of the teachers arranged their classrooms with physical designs grounded in collectivism, with clusters of desks to promote collaboration and spaces for whole group instruction. All educators used a combination of collectivist and individualist methods to reshape and reorganize their environments due to the range in student needs. As teachers gained a deeper sense of each learner, the environments evolved to reflect their awareness of the students they were serving and how they learned best. Students devised norms, pledges, and expectations in partnership with educators (Rothstein-Fisch & Trumbull, 2008). Through the project, teachers learned more about themselves and how to connect with their students, understanding that instructional strategies must align with the environment co-constructed with students and their needs in mind (Trumbull, Rothstein-Fisch, Greenfield, & Quiroz, 2001).

We can arrange spaces to convey distinct messages and serve as an invitation for learning. Reggio schools refer to their environments as a *third teacher* (Edwards, Gandini, & Forman, 1993; Wurm, 2005), a space that promotes critical thinking, communication, relationships, and creativity. As a teacher who worked in a Reggio-inspired school, I was positioned in a role to intentionally think about the language of space and messages the classroom environment communicated. I wanted my students to see themselves as readers, writers, mathematicians, creative thinkers, and lifelong learners. Importantly, I wanted students to feel as if they could bring their whole self to school and view our classroom as an affirming place. Education stores rarely received my monetary contributions as walls demonstrated stories of learning (e.g., *writing samples, artwork, student-made anchor charts, etc.*). If I wanted my students to see themselves as readers, I would ensure that my environment had a diverse selection of texts and invitational spaces that encouraged youth to get lost in a book. There were authentic materials to inspire inquiry, and I often reconfigured the room to provide more space for mobility and interactions. The décor of the physical environment validated the interests of learners, because frankly, I asked students what they would like to see in our shared space. We can strategically think about the design of space and provocations for learning that have a positive impact on student performance and psychological safety.

Brain-Compatible Spaces

Each space within a classroom environment can serve as an invitation for learning. Children are inquisitive, intellectual beings who are consistently trying to make sense of the phenomena in their life space. Gholdy Muhammad (2020) conveyed that if we want students to see and recognize their brilliance, then "they must step into schools and classrooms where intellectualism is deeply seeded, expected, and nurtured" (p. 108). The physical classroom must become brain-compatible space with objects designed to elicit provocations and a lens of criticality. Imagination and exploration are necessary for a learning-focused classroom.

Desautels and McKnight (2016) described the importance of creating a space for neuro connectivity within their book, *Unwritten: The Story of a Living System*. Classroom environments can be sites of innovation where there is space for connections and a renewed sense of self. The following excerpt from *Unwritten: The Story of a Living System*, sets the stage for the importance of brain-compatible environments:

> In many ways, our education system is often experienced by educators and students as mechanistic. We move in lines, we sit in spaces that tell us when to think, how to think, and we move in lines listening for the bells. We feel a disconnected and hollow mindset that exudes a ubiquitous air of doing, going, accomplishing, assessing, and repeating it all the very next day.
>
> (p. 21)

Intellectually engaging environments are spaces where children can develop deeper understandings of the world, formulate questions, and build connections (Curtis & Carter, 2003). Instructional materials should be viewed as a means to enhance identity development. We can be aware of theme-based décor that may over-stimulate learners and squelch creativity. Brain-compatible spaces serve as a catalyst for process-driven thinking in which students are given the opportunity to struggle productively. Identity affirming classrooms honor the brain and commemorate authentic representations of learning. Authenticity refers to human-centered work that showcases the strengths, creativity, and brilliance of learners (Lackney, Fielding, & Nair, 2013). Displays that highlight uniformity in written responses, commercialized crafts, and worksheets often disregard the authentic ways a learner can express their applications of knowledge (Campbell-Hill & Ekey, 2010). As an alternative to synthetic, workbook-related materials that stifle creativity and often condition learners how to think, students can write in journals, engage in intellectual debates, and develop illustrations of learning concepts (Campbell-Hill & Ekey, 2010). In the article, "Consider the Walls" (2004), Patricia Tarr encouraged teachers to think about the relationship between the image of learners and what is displayed in the classroom environment. Tarr's (2004) article helps us to frame the following questions for consideration:

◆ What is the purpose of featured items or materials displayed in a classroom environment?
◆ Who is acknowledged and what is celebrated within the classroom environment?
◆ What values are being communicated through the physical design of classroom space?
◆ What image of a learner is conveyed through displays of classroom materials or representations of learning?
◆ How do the classroom materials contribute to the atmosphere of the environment?
◆ How do the walls reflect the rich cultures and lived experiences of students and their caregivers?

Curtis and Carter (2003) conveyed that objects from the natural world such as rocks, shells, bird nests, and tree stumps may elicit a strong sense of exploration. Through Indigenous education, we learn that "living in the natural world provides the ideal environment of developing both the individual and the community" (Cajete, 2015, p. 28). The natural world appeals to our sensory needs. Classrooms that incorporate elements of nature (including time outdoors) intrinsically motivate students to utilize their senses. Students build schema through exploration and discoveries that involve sensory skills. Artifacts from nature demonstrate the importance of connectivity to the outside world. Students need environments where intellectual and cross-cultural engagement are stimulated via the incorporation of instructional materials that ignite critical thinking and investigations.

Brain-compatible spaces also incorporate appropriate lighting and color considerations (Lackney, Fielding, & Nair, 2013). Lackney, Fielding, and Nair (2013) imparted that learning is

connected to levels of lighting. Natural lighting positively cor-
relates to memory retrieval. Furthermore, daylight is known to
"have a calming effect on the human brain" (p. 189). Research
studies have shown "that in day-lit classrooms math scores
improve by 20% and verbal scores by 22%" (p. 160). Therefore,
weather permitted, it is important to consider times where students can learn or have a brain break in outdoor environments.
As this book was written during a global pandemic, I can affirm
the power of the outdoors for mental clarity and wellness. Colors
also impact pathways for learning as they can elicit behavioral
responses if loud or distracting. Therefore, it's important to analyze how students respond to variations in lighting and color
(Curtis & Carter, 2003; Lackney, Fielding, & Nair, 2013) via kid-
watching and discussions about their reactions to classroom
spaces.

 Mirror Work

Our bodies reside in different places daily and it's worth it to
take an intentional pause, hydrate, and reflect on the messages
we're absorbing within our surroundings. Environments can be
a whole vibe, with energy that makes us feel a sense of belonging or the need retreat (there are some places I cannot leave fast
enough). Take the time to reflect on the following questions as a
part of your self-work.

1. Name the qualities you would look for in an identity
    affirming, physical environment.
2. Where does that identity affirming place exist in your life
    based on the qualities named?
3. Think about the identity affirming space that you identi-
    fied. Answer the following questions that are applicable
    to the space you named:
    ◆ What does it look like?
    ◆ What does it feel like?
    ◆ What do you hear?

◆ What do you smell?
◆ What can you taste?

4. How has your identity and understanding of affirming spaces shaped the way you design your classroom environment? Is there a disconnect between your beliefs and construction of space?

5. What messages and beliefs does your classroom environment send to students?

Administrators may also want to think about commonly shared spaces such as the cafeteria, library, hallways, and other gathering spaces, and practice walk-throughs within buildings to assess environments (see Appendix A). *What message does the school send to current and prospective students and their families?* The environments we operate in daily have been deliberately constructed through human decisions. We hold the power to change and alter the physical context to affirm the identities and abilities of students. Create spaces for listening where you receive input from teachers, students, and caregivers. You may even develop a group (e.g., teachers, students, counselors, etc.) to conduct environment walks that evaluate the messages of space (see **Collective Work**).

Co-Constructing Spaces of Belonging

My grandmother, Levater Greer, had an antique jewelry armoire in a spare bedroom within her home. As a child, I would spend hours in that room, lost in the beauty and intricate details of each radiant piece that represented a story of the woman I profoundly admired. The room was my safe place, a space where I could breathe deeply and just be. I could feel the presence of ancestors, unconditional love, and the strength of a long history of Black women who resisted people devaluing their worth. It was a restorative realm during the summer months where I could shed the pain of erasure from school environments. While functioning in predominantly white school spaces, I yearned for the warmth I had in that small room which made me feel visible. *What was missing in my school environment? Why did school perpetuate invisibility? What could my teachers bottle up from Levater's room to affirm my existence? … To make me feel safe?*

When creating spaces of belonging, it is important to activate student voice and understand what makes youth feel seen. Representation matters. We can design spaces that serve as a mirror for culturally, linguistically, and ethnically diverse learners. While serving as a chief equity officer, Kayla Rago, a second-grade teacher, reached out to discuss a project initiated by her students. While viewing art with a teacher librarian, the students noticed that hanging portraits and wall art within the school environment portrayed mostly white people. This noticing led to a student-based movement to design wall spaces that reflected racial diversity.

The students drafted a letter to their principal, which led to the funding of a project where they worked with a parent who was a professional photographer. In partnership, the students held conversations about race, determined the images that should be represented in their school, and worked with the photographer to take pictures of peers in various locations on campus. When the canvas prints were complete, I was able to attend a ribbon-cutting ceremony where the students dedicated their portraits to the school. The project received national attention, featured in a Teacher2Teacher article titled "A Student-led Project Made our Class More Inclusive" (Rago, 2020). Students of all ages can co-construct environments with teachers and create a space that fosters positive memories.

I interviewed four students individually to learn more about their perspectives of school and classroom environments relative to identity-affirming spaces: *Laila Brown (seventh grade), Nithya Murthy (junior), Maena Ochieng (eighth grade), and Tyson Slack (eighth grade).* All students were enrolled in different schools between Indiana and Florida at the time of the interview and represent different racial, ethic, and gender identities. For context and building background knowledge, I unpacked the term "identity affirming" to help the students understand that the questions centered the notion of creating a welcoming environment. The students were asked the following questions:

1. What would you expect to see in an identity affirming classroom (welcoming environment that honors diversity, your existence, and humanity)?
2. Would you consider your classroom an identity affirming environment? Why or why not?
3. How can teachers help to create an identity affirming classroom (physical environment)? What can students do?

Question One: Expectations of an Identity Affirming Space

LAILA: It would be a diverse classroom and the teacher wouldn't pick on students if there was a question to be answered … Kids would interact with each other. In the hallways, normally in the hallways there are "No Bullying" signs or sign-ups for student clubs. I would love to see more books that address the problems in the world.

NITHYA: Around the classroom our teachers often have decorations about what they like or what interests them, so an identity affirming classroom would have more things relative to the student … such as flags from various countries or souvenirs or things like that. Every time I see things that are from Asia, like a little decorative statue or something, I'm interested in that because that has something to do with my race, the family I come from … so I find it inclusive when teachers acknowledge that their students have other cultures, races, histories, and traditions; and I like when they include that [acknowledgment] in talks in the classroom or decorations in the classroom.

TYSON: More teaching and things that demonstrate successful African Americans.

MAENA: Different posters set up in teachers' classrooms and posters that students make; and put those in the halls. There are some teachers that have rainbow flags to support people in the LGBTQ+ community to make them feel welcomed. Personally, I like when teachers wear things or show support for Black Lives Matter. I'm mixed race and it's nice to feel supported by teachers.

Question Two: Assessment of an Affirming Space

LAILA: Yes [it is a welcoming space]. In my homeroom teacher's classroom, he had some inspiriting quotes (e.g., Spread love and make a difference.) One, the quotes on the wall are encouraging. Two, the teacher (makes the space affirming) … if a teacher doesn't have people skills, they shouldn't be a teacher. Three, the spacing of the desks (e.g., semi-circle arrangement) and the kids sitting at them makes the classroom welcoming.

NITHYA: Not a lot [classrooms are not welcoming spaces]. Like Freshman year I had an AP World [class] … I had a teacher who did a great job talking about race relations. Her classroom was wonderful. It had flags from different countries. I felt so included in that classroom because she acknowledged our races and different cultures. A lot of teachers push race under the rug. Other classrooms are just a normal classroom. I'm not negatively affected in terms of my grades but do lack a connection with the teacher in those rooms. I'm not as willing to put myself out there. It's not negative, but it's not positive either. It feels like a non-affirming identity classroom is the norm so students like me are just used to it … We see identity affirming environments as extra when it should be the standard.

TYSON: Yes. We have posters in the hallways and walls. It's not like only on Black history month when we celebrate. We celebrate every day. Every day I feel like my identity is celebrated. I don't go to the library much, but I know there are a lot of books about Black people and by Black people. There's a lot of diverse books at a school like this (i.e., Spanish Immersion magnet school).

MAENA: Yes. I have teacher who has maps from different countries. It shows diversity in the classroom. There are also motivational quotes. I feel safer in that room and I can be myself. However, I don't think it's just about what a teacher puts on the walls, but how they show support.

Question 3: The Role of Educators and/or Students

LAILA: So, my teacher this year, every morning we did social emotional learning. We watched student news … Teachers should help students who need help. Trust is also important. I trust most of my teachers. It would also be helpful if students helped new students to find their footing in the classroom or in schools.

NITHYA: Teachers have a hard job. I feel like many teachers are not willing to change and do extra work to include their students of color. Because they may see that what they're doing is already good enough, I guess. Teachers don't know what I go through, what I do outside of school as related to my race or traditions (i.e., Hindu celebrations) … Teachers could try to get more in touch with students and find out more about what goes on in their lives outside of school.

TYSON: I don't know how to answer, because I don't really mind much stuff, even if it's non-affirming. I just don't take stuff to mind.

MAENA: They [teachers] can start a conversation and ask how my day is going. They can dig deeper and see how you're doing and learn more about you. They should ask how we feel safe in the classroom.

There's power in voice and listening to students' needs. Although the students identified many elements that enhance an environment and create an affirming space, it was evident that all students yearned for an authentic connection with teachers. They wanted teachers who could see their humanity and demonstrate care. An affirming, physical environment was just another way to enhance the beliefs that students already felt from teachers due their actions (see Figure 2.1).

Creating Mindful-Affirming Spaces

In Sarah Williams Goldhagen's book (2017), *Welcome to Your World: How the Built Environment Shapes our Lives*, she emphasized how architecture and the spaces people construct affect wellness and influence human experiences. As educators, we must think about the alignment between our beliefs and the spaces we create, and how the classroom shapes educational experiences. *Do students*

*question their belonging and safety in our environments? Could our phys-
ical space and designs be a hindrance for learning? What adjectives would
students use to describe how they feel in a classroom environment?* Here
are seven considerations for designing spaces of belonging:

1. Start with a blank canvas. You do not need to possess all
   the things in your classroom at the start of the year. Get to
   know your learners. Understand their interests, passions,
   and aspirations. Ask them what they would like to see in
   their classroom environment and determine how you can
   co-construct it over time together. I promise it will relieve
   the pressure of having your room set up at the beginning
   of the year.

2. Define spaces within the classroom with a clear purpose.
   Make sure that areas convey an invitation for learning.
   Think about the ways learning can be framed through
   collectivist and individualistic spaces to support identity
   development.

3. Consider the power of outdoor spaces and the impact
   on wellness. We all need to breathe and have moments
   of mindfulness, knowing the research that it helps with
   performance.

4. Be mindful of clutter and overstimulating environments
   (e.g., *visual, auditory, etc.*) that may be a distraction from
   learning.

5. Think about accessibility, specifically for students with
   disabilities who may need ramps, wide doorways, and
   other measures within a school facility. Consider creating
   spaces where students can de-escalate that incorporate
   features to enhance social emotional learning—*and no,
   I'm not referring to anything that replicates a carceral system.*
   I have visited plenty of schools that have fidget walls and
   materials that help with emotional regulation.

6. Steer clear of learning materials (e.g., *posters, displays,
   etc.*) that feature stereotypical images of the identities of
   learners and be watchful of gender binary structures or
   language that may signal exclusion within a physical
   environment.

7. Reflect on how you show up within the environment and the beliefs that are conveyed about the identities of learners. The layout and design of the classroom can shape human interactions and foster joyful memories. Mirror work is valuable. Our beliefs directly impact the environments we create and how we honor students.

As expressed in earlier chapters, educational systems are inherently inequitable, and the sociopolitical contexts of schools may impact how you construct an environment. You may read the suggestions and feel like they're far removed from your reality due to power dynamics, quantity of students (i.e., *teaching multiple course sections*), and roles that may require you to teach in different rooms throughout the instructional day. However, you have also been provided a **Systems Work** framework to address inequities with thought partners and can mobilize communities to support needs. Voice is a powerful tool to determine the makings of an affirming environment. Teachers who travel between classrooms to deliver instruction can also think about seating arrangements and authentic representations of learning as a part of instructional lessons that can be displayed throughout the school. Barriers are human-created obstacles that we can deconstruct and eliminate.

Chapter Highlights

♦ The stimuli within an environment condition responses and shape identity development.
♦ We can arrange spaces to convey distinct messages about belonging and serve as an invitation for learning.
♦ Intellectually engaging environments can help students develop deeper understandings of the world and their identity as learners.
♦ The arrangement and design of space should be approached with an equity lens. We can co-construct spaces with students that are brain-compatible, empowering, and identity affirming.

 **Collective Work**

Take an environment walk with a group of colleagues around your school building or find an accountability partner to assess your classroom environment. What messages does the physical environment send about mattering and belonging? Have a colleague(s) complete an environment walk in your classroom. *What do they notice? What do they wonder?* Create time to debrief and actively listen for understanding. Consider using the guide (RACE) in Appendix A and reflect on the following questions:

1. What does the environment invite students to learn or do based on its layout and design?
2. How does the environment foster identity development where students are able to learn more about themselves and who they are as learners?

It may be difficult to hear someone provide constructive feedback regarding a space that is considered a *home away from home*—I practically lived in my classroom as a teacher. However, feedback is needed to see what may not be visible to us. As always, this work is more effective if you and colleagues are actively engaged in mirror work—because, real talk, I wouldn't grant some colleagues the time to tell me what a classroom needs to be an identity affirming space. Work with colleagues who are also on a journey and will challenge your thinking.

References

Cajete, G. (2015). *Indigenous Community: Rekindling the Teachings of the Seventh Fire*. St. Paul, MN: Living for Justice.

Campbell-Hill, B., & Ekey, C. (2010). *The Next-Step Guide to Enriching Classroom Environments: Rubrics and Resources for Self-Evaluation and Goal Setting for Literacy Coaches, Principals, and Teacher Study Groups, K-6*. Portsmouth, NH: Heinemann.

Curtis, D., & Carter, M. (2003). *Designs for Living and Learning: Transforming Early Childhood Environments*. St. Paul, MN: Redleaf Press.

Desautels, L., & McKnight, M. (2016). *Unwritten: The Story of a Living System*. Deadwood, OR: Wyatt-MacKenzie Publishing.

Edwards, C., Gandini, L., & Forman, G. (Eds.). (1993). *The Hundred Languages of Children: The Reggio Emilia Approach to Early Childhood Education*. Norwood, NY: Ablex Publishing Co.

Goldhagen, Sarah W. (2017). *Welcome to Your World: How the Built Environment Shapes Our Lives*. New York, NY: Harper Collins.

Jackson, Philip W. (1990). *Life in Classrooms*. New York, NY: Teachers College Press.

Lackney, J., Fielding, R., & Nair, P. (2013). *The Language of School Design: Design Patterns for 21st Century Schools* (3rd ed.). Washington, DC: National Clearinghouse for Educational Facilities.

Muhammad, G. (2020). *Cultivating Genius: An Equity Framework for Culturally and Historically Responsive Literacy*. New York, NY: Scholastic.

Rago, K. (June 2020). A student-led project made our school more inclusive. *Teachers2Teachers*.www.teacher2teacher.education/2020/06/21/a-- student-led-project-made-our-school-more-inclusive/

Rothstein-Fisch, Carrie, & Trumbull, Elise. (2008). *Managing Diverse Classrooms: How to Build on Students' Cultural Strengths*. Alexandria, VA: ASCD.

Savage, T.V. (1999). *Teaching Self-Control Through Management and Discipline*. Boston, MA: Allyn & Bacon.

Tarr, P. (May 2004). Consider the walls. National Association for the Education of Young Children (NAEYC). *YC Young Children*, *59*(3), 88–92.

Trumbull, E., Rothstein-Fisch, C., Greenfield, P., & Quiroz, B. (2001). *Bridging Cultures Between Home and School: A Guide for Teachers*. Mahwah, NJ: Lawrence Erlbaum Associates.

Wurm, J.P. (2005). *Working in the Reggio Way: A Beginner's Guide for American Teachers*. St. Paul, MN: Redleaf Press.

5

Humanizing Approaches and the Power of Community

Humility gives us space to see that we do not have all the answers, even in our so-called areas of expertise; it lets us listen and respond to what is actually happening, being said, and being felt.

Derrick Bell (2002, p. 165)

What does it mean to be human? It's a simple question that is often neglected when we are subjected to demands, expectations, and responsibilities that come with the ebbs and flows of life. Being a human involves carrying a wide range of emotions. We feel joy, anger, grief, happiness, sadness, and a combination of sentiments simultaneously. Through hardships, there's an unveiling of inner strength. We learn how to be resilient, bouncing back from despair and finding hope.

Being human is a desire to be in community with others. The affirmatory connections we establish fuel the soul and provide peace. Through our relationships, we acquire understandings of compassion, vulnerability, and positionality. We figure out our place in the world while making mistakes along the way. There are times we will get things wrong before making them right. We will experience guilt and shame, walking away from spaces that are harmful and no longer serve a purpose. There will be

DOI: 10.4324/9781003216964-8

moments when we hurt people, perhaps individuals we care about the most. We learn how to make amends and forgive. And through it all, we find the capacity to love.

Humanizing approaches come from a place of love. *It's understanding* the human condition that youth bring into the classroom environment. *It's recognizing* that everyone has imperfections while made with promise. *It's acknowledging* that mishaps will be made and offering grace. When our praxis reflects love, we fight fiercely for children and advocate for their needs. Human work requires us to think about how we show up for students.

> We cannot lose sight of what it means to be human while working with youth.

 **Mirror Work**

Being human is a story in motion. It's the feeling we get when laughter is shared from an inside joke to the ugly cry released from a tragic event or painful memory—the funeral scene from the movie, My Girl, gets me every time on sight. Think about what it means to be human. Personalize it. Describe the beauty and complexities of your humanity. What does it mean to just be? The following reflective questions may give you a jumpstart of ponderings to process:

- ◆ Write about your human condition. How do you see yourself or process your own emotions? Are you in touch with how you feel? How are you feeling at this moment?
- ◆ How do the spaces you operate in (e.g., workplace, social circles, etc.) consider your humanity?
- ◆ What actions from others affirm your humanity and make you feel seen?

Honestly, I have struggled with some of these questions which is indicative of an unbalanced work life. I know there are more days than not when I have abandoned myself and my own needs while striving to take care of students, colleagues, friends, and family. If you look at these questions and you don't even know where to begin or how to feel, you may likely be in a position (like me) where you forget or fail to pour into yourself. While fighting relentlessly for others, make sure to take care of yourself. Being human involves intentional pauses and restorative rest. We cannot give our all while dismissing our own needs.

Understanding Emotions

Human development involves us learning how to effectively manage and process our emotions. In Thich Nhat Hanh's (1991) *Peace is in Every Step*, we are reminded that "our feelings play a very important part in directing all of our thoughts and actions" (p. 51). Interpersonal relationships are challenging to maintain if one lacks the skills to problem-solve, self-regulate, and empathize with others. As a part of our human condition, there will be voids in understanding that must be filled with knowledge through explicit modeling and teaching. Therefore, we cannot expect that students will be equipped to employ social-emotional skills upon arrival and need to focus on how we prepare students to become better humans.

Scholar of K-12 mathematics education, Hemavibushani Khodai (2021), shared in a journal for the National Council of Teachers of Mathematics that "belonging is not bestowed, it is created" (p. 556). Students need opportunities where they can practice empathy and sound decision-making, understanding how they respond and interact with others in different contexts. Social emotional learning (SEL) is not a new concept despite the national attention—*positive and negative*—the pedagogy has garnered in recent years. It is clear that the anti-SEL groups who argue, pack school board rooms, and hold protesting signs stating that teachers should only focus on *reading, writing, and arithmetic* have never navigated the social dynamics of a classroom. There has not been a day in my years of teaching or while serving as a school administrator when I have not had to alter plans to work on interpersonal or social skills with students—*I won't even get into all of the TikTok and social media challenges that have placed me in a position to support schools.* Educators have been accustomed to helping students achieve goals, make sound decisions, and navigate struggles productively. The Collaborative for Academic, Social, and Emotional Learning (CASEL) has emphasized the importance of teaching competencies such as *self-awareness, self-management, social awareness, relationship skills,* and *responsible decision-making.* There are more than 200 different SEL programs that exist globally, and evaluative tools are available (i.e., *Ecological Approaches to Social Emotional Learning funded by the Wallace Foundation*) to analyze frameworks (Khodai, 2021). SEL helps students and adults acquire the artistry needed to generate a cohesive, affirming community across academic settings.

However, the strategies and lessons that accompany each competency must be taught with a race-conscious lens in an environment where educational equity is prioritized. Founder of LiberatED, Dena Simmons (2019), asserted that SEL is merely "white supremacy with a hug" if it is taught in absence of sociopolitical and racial contexts, particularly when working with racialized groups. It is counterproductive to teach SEL skills in an environment that induces trauma. Rather, SEL should "feel like healing from trauma and grief for Indigenous, Black, racialized, and otherwise marginalized students and educators, who experience oppression and racial trauma in schools and classrooms themselves" (Khodai, 2021, p. 557). It should not be employed as a method control, but as a means to help students build "a healthy individual and collective identity" (Khodai, 2021, p. 557). The effectiveness of SEL strategies are contingent upon the equitable conditions within a learning environment.

In the process of examining emotions and providing scaffolds for students, it's necessary to also think about positionality, vulnerability, and the impact of trauma. We need to be cognizant of the ways power and privilege affect social identities and classroom experiences. *Do students view their classrooms as a welcoming space that honors their full humanity?* With a lens of criticality, we must question if classrooms are psychologically safe environments for risk-taking and authentic connections.

Positionality

Our identities are socially constructed within a system of power that influences the way we operate in the world and the emotions we bring into experiences. Positionality is the idea that identities are relational and fluid positions that can be analyzed as people shift social contexts (Maher & Tetreault, 2001; Martin & Gunten, 2002). One's navigation is influenced by the power inherent in social positions. Positionality refers to the recognition of one's location in societal systems in relation to others and understanding how one's position shapes the way they engage with society (Misawa, 2010). Through the understanding of positionality, we gain insight of other peoples' perspectives and experiences while functioning in an unjust world. We learn how to re-examine our actions and consciously think about how we show up or position ourselves in different group dynamics.

Vulnerability

Learning partnerships reflect trusting, meaningful relationships. When we feel trust, we become emotionally connected and invested in personal growth (Brown, 2018). As humans, we will make mistakes and misread the situations we encounter. Fear may suppress the words that need to be lifted as well as the feelings that should be released. Vulnerability exposes emotions, causing us to face discomfort.

Derrick Bell (2002), one of the originators of CRT, asserted that "humility gives us space to see that we do not have all the answers, even in our so-called areas of expertise; it lets us listen and respond to what is actually happening, being said, and being felt" (p. 165). Vulnerability means that we may not have the answer or an adequate response, yet we're open to new perspectives and guidance with the notion that there is much to comprehend within this thing called life. I have learned that I cannot expect students to share their humanity with me if I'm unwilling to be vulnerable. There's a need to create conditions

> When we step into the unknown and embrace vulnerability, we find courage, strength, and our wholly authentic selves.

that encourage vulnerability and brave spaces where students are freely able to express themselves.

Trauma

There are times when the manifestation of stress or disturbing circumstances profoundly obstruct our body's ability to cope. Trauma affects our neurological health and physical wellness, causing emotions that include but are not limited to anxiety, rage, depression, feelings of uncertainty, or mistrust (Menakem, 2017). Not everyone is equipped to address trauma or has access to measures for healing, which significantly impacts perception, and the way people approach situations in their lived experiences. The trauma attached to our bodies may communicate that certain individuals (e.g., *based on attributes, personality, or words expressed*) or environments are not safe, which draws tangled emotional responses.

Some students (adults too) enter the classroom with a history of traumatic experiences. They are hypervigilant and on-guard with every encounter or change with the belief that someone or something may pose as a source of danger. Trauma may cause students to become emotionally withdrawn or distracted with an inclination to avoid people or responsibilities. Sometimes the body compounds trauma with other emotionally wounding and unhealed experiences which have a lasting effect on the brain and causes responses unimaginable to who one believes to be (Menakem, 2017). My early years of teaching often resembled a relay race as certain students triggered from unhealed trauma would sprint out of the classroom as a coping mechanism. I have also worked with students who immediately resorted to violence as opposed to a restorative conversation.

> Every behavior communicates a message from a chapter of someone's life".

Alex Shevrin Venet's (2021) *Equity-Center Trauma-Informed Education* described how educators should consider the fostering of predictability, flexibility, empowerment, and connection when making trauma-informed decisions. Youth experiencing trauma need flexible routines, predictable and thoughtful responses, connections to caring and self-regulated adults, and empowering student-centered practices (Venet, 2021). As educators, being trauma-informed requires us to be vigilant, flexible, and responsive to the needs of students with an understanding of trauma and how it operates within bodies.

Importantly, we also have to recognize that school environments can also be the origin of trauma or retraumatize students. In the Learning for Justice article, "Ending Curriculum Violence" (2020), Stephanie Jones discussed how curriculum can harm the well-being of learners. Scholars Erhabor Ighodaro and Greg Wiggan (2013) coined the term curriculum violence to describe how academic programming can jeopardize psychological safety and cause trauma. During most of my early childhood years, teachers would spend half a day teaching false narratives about Thanksgiving and dressed me up as a colonizer. As I grew older and learned more about Indigenous history and the dehumanizing acts that took place in residential schools (*as we continue to learn about the unmarked graves of over a thousand Indigenous people, mostly children within Canada in 2021*), the elementary memories and pictures haunted me—*and I still don't understand why many schools actively engage in that practice today*. Oppression is not an event or a costume. When I think about my eighth-grade year, the first thing that comes to mind is the curriculum violence I experienced while being forced to watch the series *Roots* (1977), with no trigger warnings or debriefing. I remember scenes of enslaved Africans, including Kunta Kinte, being brutally beaten and feeling eyes on my back from white peers in class. My high school orchestra teacher deemed playing hip-hop on the violin inappropriate, so of course, I had to rebel and play Biggie instead of Bach at a school convocation. All these experiences and approaches from educators were harmful, and not what I expected from a place responsible for my care. Jones (2020) developed a database called *Mapping Racial Trauma in Schools*, which tracks curriculum violence within schools. In 2021, numerous schools have been in a national spotlight for malpractices in the form of curriculum violence:

◆ In Wyncote, Pennsylvania at Bishop McDevitt High School, a criminal justice class assignment provided prompts regarding the Derek Chauvin trial. One of the prompts conveyed that George Floyd's death was due to drug consumption that affected his heart and asked students to write whether Chauvin should be charged with murder if he did not directly kill him (Thomas, 2021).

♦ In San Juan Unified School District an English teacher from Rio Americano High School displayed a Nazi war flag during class (Townsend & Torre, 2021).

♦ Two Black students in Spokane, Washington were directed to clean picked cotton for a classroom assignment at Sacajawea Middle School (Geranios, 2021).

♦ During a Zoom class a teacher in a Sacramento school district made disparaging gestures toward Asian Americans by making her eyes slanted and describing how the shape of eyes determines ethnicity. A voice on the recording yelled, *"I should leave your class right now."*

♦ A student from Julliard reported a workshop called Slavery Saturday where the class was instructed to pretend to be *"slaves as a guest speaker played audio of whips, rain, and racial slurs"* (CBS, 2021).

♦ Following national Black Lives Matter protests in 2020, many students in K-12 environments as well as collegiate levels (including places where I have either worked or attended as a student) developed "Black At" accounts on Instagram as a platform to talk about acts of racism on school campuses. Many students continue to add stories to these accounts (Smith-Barrow, 2020).

In my work of creating liberatory spaces, I recognize that I'm a survivor of many traumatic events from my K-12 as well as collegiate level experiences. The relationship dynamics in a classroom may affect students psychologically if identity threats are present, including bullying and harassment. As a district-level Title IX coordinator, I have seen the impact school systems have on students when the education of discriminatory practices, procedures for reporting sexual harassment, support services, and accountability measures to ensure a safe culture and climate are lacking. Therefore, the **Systems Work** (see Chapter 2) is a critical, ongoing process that names the identity threats that are harmful to students. If we can name it, we can dismantle it.

Decolonize Your Mind and Classroom

A third-grade teacher attempted to take a brown crayon out of my hand and exchange it for a peach color after she noticed my depiction of Jesus as a Black man—*yes, a lot of Crayola curriculum back in those days.* Little did the teacher know, my house was full of Black Jesus (and Santa too) as my mom collected figurines, and I was also intelligent enough at the age of nine to know that a dark pigment (despite all the pale, fair-skinned images of Jesus in school) would be evident in a biblical story that took place near the equator. Yet, this teacher was passionate about "correcting me" and set a standard for my work due to her social construction. She deliberately overlaid her adopted norms over my reality.

The emotions and practices we bring into the classroom are a product of our experiences. Due to the nature of living in an unjust world that upholds forms of oppression within every system, many of us have been socialized to adopt norms while existing in spaces under the confines of whiteness. Many of the systems, policies, and procedures developed by humans in positions of power reflect the ways they have been conditioned to see and live in the world. Therefore, we must interrogate the dominant ideologies and how whiteness influences the spaces we design for children. Teachers also hold power over the decisions made in the classroom. *We can* determine the content and supplemental materials that need to be taught, and co-construct learning experiences with students. *We can* honor the native languages, culture, and racial experiences of students within the classroom, having critical conversations about social justice. *We can* help students to see that there are different methods to showing proficiency. To hold power means that we also have to engage in a practice of ideological unlearning.

One of my most powerful teachable moments occurred during my first year of teaching. While administering a math journal problem to a group of kindergarten students, I was approached by a student who was eager to show me her results. The problem read as followed:

> Miss Buchanan only has four chairs in her home. She invited Sydnee, Ashton, Arius, and Jacob over for a snack. Will there be enough chairs for everyone, including Miss Buchanan, to sit down and enjoy the snack?

Sydnee solved the problem and shared that there would be enough seats for everyone. Immediately, this innate non-negotiable feeling emerged, and I advised that she may need to rethink her problem and try it again. The student continued to share that she was confident in her response and came up with a solution. I proceeded to demonstrate multiple strategies that matched my thinking. And again, Sydnee conveyed that there were enough seats because she figured out a way to make things work. Baffled by her reasoning, I took the time to meticulously look at her illustration as all students were required to demonstrate their problem-solving methods. In a combination of lowercase and capital letters she wrote, "Jacob cAnt coM." Then, Sydnee proceeded to explain that she uninvited a student due to the lack of chairs available so we could all have a place to sit.

Her math journal taught me a valuable lesson about the importance of decolonizing my mind. I started to question: *How often do I expect students to fit their thinking into a box that I created? How did I create this box? Why do I hold the notion that things need to be executed in a certain way to meet standards? Where did these standards originate from? How are these standards harming the creativity and brilliance of the students I'm serving, particularly those at the margins?* While attempting to have Sydnee match my reasoning, I had failed to match *her* thinking process and see the possibilities beyond the way I conceptualized the problem.

Decolonizing our minds is a process of unlearning where we deconstruct the ideologies and binaries that other individuals, repress cultures, or deem people as inadequate due to the categorical, socially constructed hierarchies embedded in thinking—*sometimes, without even knowing*. The advancement of educational equity is a combination of mirror work and systems work where we collectively assess and challenge the power structures that yield unequal outcomes. We must understand the role we play in maintaining inequities. When you think of success, how do you define it and are those views tied to your expectations of students? (Kawi, 2020). In Hahnville High School in Boutte, Louisiana (Page, 2021) a student was prohibited from graduating due to the style of shoes he was wearing (which led to a teacher providing the student his own shoes). How were those standards for a dress code determined? A policy that would cost a significant milestone and accomplishment for a student? Considering the subjective nature of disciplinary offenses such as disruption and insubordination, how are we decolonizing our minds when working with human behaviors? The decolonization process starts with us (mirror work), and then we work to develop content with essential identity questions (Chapter 3) in a physical environment (Chapter 4) that is designed to value the identity of students.

Developing a Learning Community

Community is fundamental to humanity and an entry point to understanding how our liberation is tied together. "Changing oppression begins with developing confidence, and confidence grows as we learn new skills through research and education-again, both personally and communally" (Cajete, 2015, p. 129). Carl Rogers, a humanistic psychologist, claimed that we learn more about ourselves through discourse with others. Connectivity to others and relationships we establish are important to our survival, helping us to become fully functioning humans who feel, seek challenges and new experiences, and appreciate learning (Rogers & Farson, 1957). When we are a part of a community, we share a story that blends into our personal history. Through community, we learn about justice and love. Therefore, in our work with students we must consider how a community is built and sustained with care for human development (Figure 5.1).

Human work centers humanity in the spaces we create. Building community requires us to question how we care for human beings, their intellect, and well-being. All members of a

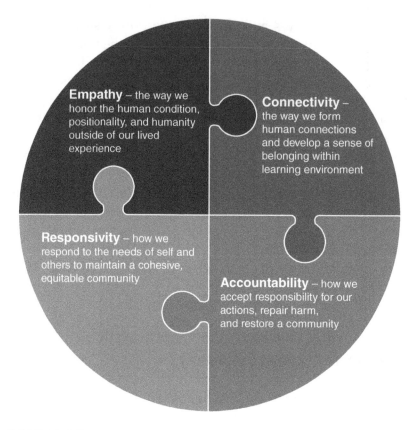

FIGURE 5.1 Collective CARE in Classrooms

community are connected and responsible for a culture of care within their environments. Human care in the classroom and beyond invites us to think about the following:

Connectivity—the way we form human connections and develop a sense of belonging within learning environment.

Accountability—how we accept responsibility for our actions, repair harm, and restore a community.

Responsivity—how we respond to the needs of self and others to maintain a cohesive, equitable community.

Empathy—the way we honor the human condition, positionality, and humanity outside of our lived experience.

Human connections can happen organically or through structured opportunities for socialization. As a teacher, I often kid-watched to document and make mental notes of the personalities and interests of students. I watched how students interacted with peers, how they engaged in lessons, and noted their passions as signaled through their expressions when describing a topic of interest. Those observations were used to inform the formation of partnerships (e.g., pairings, small groups, conferences, etc.), social experiences, and how I designed the physical space to foster a sense of belonging. Paulo Freire (2005) conveyed in *Teachers as Cultural Workers: Letters to Those Who Dare to Teach*, that educators must be cognizant of what happens in the world through the eyes of children. We cannot be in community with people if we do not take the time to understand their needs and how life is lived.

As I write this book, students are living and operating in a global pandemic. They have witnessed national protests in support of Black lives and anti-LGBTQ+ legislations, grappled with anti-Asian violence and mass shootings, viewed images of an insurrection at the US Capitol building, and processed how multiple systems failed to protect Ma'Khia Bryant hours after the Derek Chauvin verdict for the murder of George Floyd. Simultaneously and globally, the military coup in Southeast Asia (Myanmar), surges of COVID-19 in India, and national protests to free Palestinians have also weighed heavily on the hearts, minds, and conversations of youth, particularly students who have familial ties to the locations and communities involved. While shining a light on these tragedies, I also recognize that there were many other events and experiences that were not named that children internalized. There are many disheartening headlines about death, abuse, injustice, missing persons, and natural disasters that deeply impact people and communities daily. The wave of protests and backlash against CRT, SEL, and literature that affirms gender identity or sexual orientation in schools also significantly impacts the mental health of children who are affected by the ideologies and behaviors of adults. We cannot ignore sociopolitical contexts and how the happenings within the world affect the emotional well-being of students, including their social construction. Consequently, we cannot ignore that many students are trying to figure out how to heal, cope, and process their emotions in a world full of constant suffering.

Spaces for listening and dialogue are catalysts for connectivity. When given time to engage in active listening, we see each other as humans with different capabilities, strengths, and aspirations. Connections are also built through storytelling as students develop empathy through their reflections of others' experiences. We connect through our stories and the emotions we carry in our existence. In the book *Indigenous Community: Rekindling the Teachings of the Seventh Fire* (2015), Tewa scholar and professor, Gregory Cajete stated that through the remembrance of stories we reclaim parts of our lives. Providing time and spaces for collaboration (e.g., teacher to student, student to student, etc.) helps us to see the strength in collectivism and ourselves. We see our power. Using strategies where students debrief or turn and talk to share learning experiences, can drive personal growth and development. Let students talk, analyze group dynamics, and create opportunities that position students to be learning partners.

Students and teachers, as learning partners, can additionally co-construct commitments toward sustaining a cohesive community that reflect their maintenance of a culture that supports academic, social, and emotional growth. These commitments could include active listening, monitoring biases in interactions, or *keeping it one hundred*. Students value truth. Also, notice how I have often used the term co-construct. When you co-construct commitments or agreements, it sends a message that it is not solely the onus of students to develop a sense of community. As emphasized, adults must think about how they show up, and engage in mirror and systems work that are necessary for just conditions where communities thrive.

Humanizing practices involve accountability where members of a community are held responsible for their actions and harm is repaired. As captured in previous chapters, we must explicitly teach what we expect to see and provide students the tools to navigate challenges productively. However, as a part of our human condition, there will be times when boundaries are crossed, threatening ideologies emerge, and mistakes will be made. Accountability positions individuals who caused harm to amend and restore the environment. Collectively, we disrupt harmful ideologies and actions, and utilize restorative practices. Holding students accountable means that we also look in the mirror ourselves.

As members of a community, it is vital to understand the needs that exist within shared spaces *and* exhibit responsiveness. Ubuntu is a core African belief that "the individual exists only in relationship to the collective" (Davis, 2019, p. 17). One of the most insightful professional development opportunities I experienced was led by activist and civil rights attorney, Fania Davis. She started the session with a traditional greeting of the Maasai people, stating "Casserian Njera" to an audience of educators based in Indianapolis, Indiana. The translation from the Maa language stated, *"How are the children?"* Davis (2018) explained that at the heart of Indigenous tribes is collectivism, where members of a community see themselves as interconnected with a responsibility to care for each other. The advancement of Indigenous societies was contingent upon the investment in children. An investment refers to the time, talent, and emotional energy we devote toward a purpose of great magnitude. Community is prioritized in Indigenous culture and members are responsive to the needs of all, particularly those challenged with vulnerabilities (Cajete, 2015). When we are responsive to the needs of children we invest in our pedagogical approaches, learning partnerships, and education to become what youth need us to be.

I left that experience pondering how the political landscape of education would evolve if people centered—*like really centered with no platitudes*—the well-being of children in decision-making (e.g., not their ego, politics, ideologies, meritocracy, savior complex, etc.) and responded accordingly based on their needs (i.e., like not forcing students to take standardized assessments among many other things during a global pandemic). Being responsive to needs calls us to think about the ways we demonstrate care for each other.

How can we care for each other in this environment?

How can we encourage each other during challenging circumstances?

How can we create a space that honors the human condition and the emotions that are a part of our being?

How can we acknowledge the histories and strengths of community members to foster a sense of belonging?

Empathy is another component of a cohesive, caring community. In Chapter 3, the importance of building empathy was covered, and a tool was provided with reflective questions to help you think about classroom culture. There are different types of empathy including cognitive and emotional (Goleman, 2005, 2008). Cognitive empathy refers to knowing how a person feels and processing what the individual is internalizing. Emotional empathy allows one to feel what others are experiencing, or, as Brene Brown (2018) has captured in her work, one feels with people who are affected. Empathy is not a universal response for all people. There are individuals who possess unhealed trauma or live with cognitive or emotional disabilities who have difficulty empathizing in situations. Therefore, we cannot enter human work expecting that all students should automatically know how to process their feelings, or relate and connect to others' experiences. Empathy takes intentional practice and modeling.

Restorative Practices

Since the 1970s, school data has revealed an increase in the use of suspensions as a means for behavioral modification (Losen & Skiba, 2010). Zero tolerance policies and carceral systems in schools have heightened racial disparities within educational and judicial systems, leading to studies that have renamed American schools as the pipeline to prison (Huff & Teske, 2010). The notion that punishment via punitive measures ameliorates behavioral outcomes is a fallacy due to the lack of substantial evidence (Losen & Skiba, 2010). A study from Yale Child Study Center (Bender, 2016) demonstrated that teachers (racially diverse and within preschool settings) spent more time tracking the behaviors of Black male students. The US Department of Education Office of Civil Rights reported in 2016 that Black preschool students are 3.6 times more likely to be suspended from school than white counterparts. Monique W. Morris' book *Pushout: The Criminalization of Black Girls in Schools* (2018) discussed the disproportionate rate at which Black girls are disciplined, due to racial biases and ideologies that adultify them. In an Education Week video, Terri Watson (2016) stated that the challenge is not about how we change Black girls (*not about fixing people*), but how we make sure spaces celebrate, respect, and view them as assets as opposed to problems (*addressing the system*). Accountability does not have to yield to punishment or marginalization. Rather, youth could be afforded spaces for healing unresolved trauma, learning, and restoration.

How are the children? The workshop facilitated by Fania Davis (2018) was designed to enhance comprehension of restorative justice. Davis discussed the racist and deficit ideologies of European colonialists who believed Indigenous societies were maladjusted since their lives were not guided by written word rooted in white supremacy culture. To Indigenous communities, communal relationships are the nexus of protection and generational prosperity. Instead of resorting to punitive measures to address human conditions, one could teach, re-instill necessary skills, and redress harm. When you are a part of a community, you respect the people who share a membership to that community while being held accountable to sustaining communal bonds.

Restorative justice centers the belief that humans are capable of change when given the opportunity to learn coupled with will. There is an emphasis on building relationships, accountability, and reparative actions (Davis, 2019). Restorative practices may include mechanisms that promote SEL, community service, circles for reconciliation, or peer mediation where students position themselves in a leadership role to resolve conflict. Circles provide a space for listening. It's a dialogic process that involves a facilitator (e.g., teacher, counselor, administrator, etc.) helping youth to identify their role in harm and the restoration process. Students are reminded that they are accountable to a community and utilize their voice in problem-solving. Humanizing approaches focus on relationships, including how we build and repair connections.

When the hamster formerly known as a class pet flew across the classroom at the hands of a student and died instantly upon landing—*you can't make this stuff up in the day and lives of teachers*— I could have easily lost my cool and reacted punitively with an office referral to remove the student or offered some form of punishment. Yet, the student was an integral part of our community and needed to be a part of the healing process. I also recognized that a separation would have made the student's integration back into class difficult if an attempt to repair harm was absent of their voice. Therefore, we talked about the situation in a community circle and deconstructed the commonly shared theory (of a few kindergarten students who supported the epic throw) that the hamster's ball would protect the creature inside when launched by force. And they were remorseful and mortified when finding out otherwise. To redress the situation, the students suggested the creation of a ceremony to honor their class pet, which turned into a day-project with rich literacy activities. They were working and healing collectively together, being in community with each other.

Students will make mistakes and are not exempted from poor decision-making. Therefore, the proactive work of building trust and connections is foundational to an identity affirming space. As educators, we also must reflect on our positionality and the ways we respond to needs. And through it all, the centering of humanity cannot be neglected as we care for others.

Chapter Highlights

◆ When centering humanity in our work, we intentionally need to think about what it means to be human, considering vulnerability, positionality, and the impact of trauma.
◆ The sustenance of a community requires a culture of CARE (e.g., *connectivity, accountability, responsivity, and empathy*).

♦ Accountability does not have to equate to marginalization or punitive messages. Youth need spaces for connection, learning, and healing unresolved trauma. Through restorative practices, students learn how to sustain communal bonds and redress harm.

 **Collective Work**

Part One: Examining Classrooms and School Environments

Within a professional group dynamic (e.g., *grade level team, school improvement committee, equity-related team, professional learning community, etc.*) discuss how you create a community of CARE within your school environment. Describe what the following areas look like on the chart below (Figure 5.2).

Human CARE tenets	Evidence of CARE Name how each component is demonstrated in the classroom and school environment.	Impact of CARE How do you know if your efforts are positively impacting students? What are the outcomes?
Connectivity	*Describe the ways you or students form human connections and develop a sense of belonging.*	**Things to consider…** *connections with historically marginalized groups, community stakeholders, classroom dynamics, relationships, etc.*
Accountability	*Describe how responsibility is accepted, how harm is repaired, how love is felt, and the lessons that are instilled within students to restore and sustain a sense of community on a classroom and school level.*	**Things to consider…** *student feedback, discipline data, policies, etc.*
Responsivity	*Describe how you respond to the needs within the classroom and how students respond to each other to maintain a cohesive community.*	**Things to consider…** *student voice, parent, or caregiver surveys for community feedback, etc.*
Empathy	*Describe how you and students honor the human condition and humanity in classroom and school spaces.*	**Things to consider…** *Culture of Empathy Assessment (see Chapter 3)*

FIGURE 5.2 Building a Community of CARE

Reflect on your school policies. Is accountability based on love for humanity or the colonizers who are living rent-free in the minds of decision-makers? As a collective, how do you respond to the needs of students? What does your data indicate about your culture of CARE?

Part Two: Examining Professionalism and Team Dynamics

Think about the **Mirror Work** reflection questions in this chapter. **Revisit this question:** *How do the spaces you operate in (e.g., workplace, social circles, etc.) consider your humanity?* Using the same Community of CARE tool, reflect on your work environment. Is CARE exhibited within your grade level team, among colleagues, or relationships with supervisors (e.g., principals, department chairs, central office, etc.)? *How might the perceptions of CARE vary across identities?* I have worked in schools where I have not felt connected due to the racial biases or racism … and I left those environments. Consider your needs and what you're experiencing in the workplace. Are staff members connected? Is there empathy demonstrated as a whole human who is teaching in a global pandemic? What does accountability look like? Are members of your school community responsive to each others' needs? No one is holding you back from choosing you, if needed.

References

Bell, D. (2002). *Ethical Ambition*. New York, NY: Bloomsbury.

Bender, M. (2016, October 4). Yale study tests implicit bias of preschool teachers. *Yale News.* https://yaledailynews.com/blog/2016/10/04/yale-study-tests-implicit-bias-of-preschool-teachers/

Brown, B. (2018). *Dare to Lead: Brave work. Tough Conversations. Whole Hearts.* New York, NY: Penguin Random House.

Cajete, G. (2015). *Indigenous Community: Rekindling the Teachings of the Seventh Fire.* St. Paul, MN: Living for Justice.

CBS (2021, May 26). *Juilliard School Criticized for Lack of Diversity and "Slavery" Workshop: "Those are Things that Still Live in My Mind".* www.cbsnews.com/news/juilliard-school-race-diversity-concerns/

Collaborative for Academic, Social, and Emotional Learning (CASEL). (2020). SEL: What are the core competence areas and where are they promoted? *CASEL*. https://casel.org/what-is-sel/

Davis, F. (2018, February 8). *What is Restorative Justice? [Educator Workshop]*. Indianapolis, IN: Administrative Services Center, Pike Township Schools.

Davis, F. (2019). *The Little Book of Race and Restorative Justice: Black Lives, Healing, and US Social Transformation*. New York, NY: Good Books.

Freire, P. (2005). *Teachers as Cultural Works: Letters to Those Who Dare to Teach*. Boulder, CO: Westview Press.

Geranios, N. (2021, June 2). *Family: Black Students in Washington Upset by School Project*. Associated Press. www.news10.com/news/national/family-black-students-in-washington-upset-by-school-project/

Goleman, D. (2005). *Emotional Intelligence: Why it Matters more than IQ?* New York, NY: Bantam Dell.

Goleman, D. (2008, March 1). How to help: When can empathy move us to action? *Greater Good Science Center*. https://greatergood.berkeley.edu/article/item/hot_to_help

Hanh, Thich N. (1991). *Peace is Every Step: The Path of Mindfulness in Everyday Life*. New York, NY: Bantam Books.

Huff, B.J., & Teske, S.C. (2010) The dichotomy of judicial leadership: Working with the community to improve outcomes for status youth. *Journal of Juvenile and Family Court*, *61*(2), 54–60.

Ighodaro, E., & Wiggan, G. (2013). *Curriculum Violence: America's New Civil Rights Issue (Education in a Competitive and Globalizing World)*. Hauppauge, NY: Nova Novinka.

Jones, S. (2020). Ending curriculum violence. *Learning for Justice* 64. www.learningforjustice.org/magazine/spring-2020/ending-curriculum-violence?fbclid=IwAR3RAGEVazo0wkBgA3aQzJ9D93yq9-ZbffPvWK70CvbUC3hAnZR4lis1bf0

Kawi, T. (2020, August 3). Decolonizing our classrooms starts with us. *PBS*. www.pbs.org/education/blog/decolonizing-our-classrooms-starts-with-us

Khodai, H. (2021). Ear to the ground: Belonging through social emotional learning. *Mathematics Teacher: Learning and Teaching PK-12*, *144*(7), 556–559.

Losen, D.J., & Skiba, R.J. (2010). Suspended education: Urban middle schools in crisis. *UCLA: The Civil Rights Project/Proyecto Derechos Civiles*. https://escholarship.org/uc/item/8fh0s5dv

Maher, F.A., & Tetreault, M.K.T. (2001). *The Feminist Classroom: Dynamics of Gender, Race, and Privilege* (expanded ed.). New York, NY: Rowman & Littlefield.

Martin, R.J., & Gunten, D.M. (2002). Reflected identities: Applying positionality and multicultural social reconstructionism in teacher education. *Journal of Teacher Education, 53*(1), 44–54.

Menakem, R. (2017). *My Grandmother's Hands: Racialized Trauma and the Pathway Mending Our Hearts and Bodies*. Las Vegas, NV: Central Recovery Press.

Misawa, M. (2010). Queer race pedagogy for educators in higher education: Dealing with power dynamics and positionality of LGBTQ students of color. *International Journal of Critical Pedagogy, 3*(1), 26–35.

Morris, M. (2018). *Pushout: The Criminalization of Black Girls in Schools*. New York, NY: The New Press.

Office of Civil Rights. (2016, June 7). *Key Data Highlights on Equity and Opportunity Gaps in Our Nations' Public Schools*. US Department of Education. www2.ed.gov/about/offices/list/ocr/docs/2013-14-first-look.pdf

Page, Syndy. (2021, June 1). A student was barred from graduation for wearing the wrong shoes. So a teacher gave him the shoes off his own feet. *The Washington Post*. www.washingtonpost.com/lifestyle/2021/06/01/graduation-dress-shoes-student/

Rogers, C., & Farson, R. (1957). *Active Listening*. Chicago, IL: University of Chicago.

Simmons, D. (2019). Why we can't afford whitewashed social-emotional learning. *ASCD*. Why_We_Can't_Afford_Whitewashed_Social-Emotional_Learning.aspx

Skiba, Russell, & Sprague, Jeffery. (2008, September). Safety without suspensions. *Educational Leadership, 66*, 38–43.

Smith-Barrow, D. (2020). Black at Instagram accounts put campus racism on display. Hechinger report. https://hechingerreport.org/black-at-instagram-accounts-put-campus-racism-on-display/

Thomas, T. (2021, April 28). *High School Class Assignment About Derek Chauvin Trial Sparks Controversy*. https://6abc.com/education/

class-assignment-about-derek-chauvin-trial-sparks-controversy-/10554672/

Townsend, M., & Torre, J. (2021, May 19). *Rio Americano High School Teacher on a Leave Over Displaying Nazi Flag in Classroom.* https://fox40.com/news/local-news/rio-americano-high-school-teacher-on-leave-over-displaying-nazi-flag-in-classroom/

Venet, A. (2021). *Equity-Center Trauma-Informed Education.* New York, NY: Norton & Company Inc.

Watson, T. (2016). On Black girls, discipline, and schools. *Education Week.* www.youtube.com/watch?v=MY4O96EN4to

6

Authentic Student Expressions

The power behind student advocacy groups in high schools and universities boils down to two things—freedom and focus.

Mustafaa Munir, Student

An identity affirming classroom is a student-centered environment where the contributions, reflections, and feedback from youth are celebrated and encouraged. Equity actuates when we create spaces for listening and learning. There's power in speaking truth and expressing authenticity. Language is a transformative tool of justice-centered work and source of freedom. When ideas are expressed through language, we learn more about our identity as well as the strengths and needs within a collective. Providing space for students to share experiences, process inquiries, and build community shapes a context of belonging when mindful of mirror and systems work. If we want to understand how students are internalizing and existing in school spaces, we have to amplify all forms of communication (e.g., voice, writing, art, storytelling, etc.) and consistently seek feedback from youth.

Through systems work we can interrogate policies and procedures that contradict affirming environments. However, I do not commit to that work in a silo or solely with the input of adults working within an institution. If I want a comprehensive view of the systemic nature of educational inequities, I seek

DOI: 10.4324/9781003216964-9

information from students as well as their caregivers. The work we put into the field of education is a service that needs reviews from those who partake in the experiences provided. Chapter 3 offered questions for consideration while working with students (e.g., How does the classroom environment *honor humanity?*). We can ask specific questions about needs through the format of personalized conferences, listening tours, or the development of student affinity or advocacy groups.

Conferencing

As a teacher who incorporated workshop methodology in peda-gogical approaches, conferencing became a natural way to gain student feedback and understand the progression of learners. Yet, one-to-one conferencing does not have to be housed only in a block of literacy or related to academic content. In the book, *We Got This* (2019), Cornelius Minor explained the following about meetings purposed to maintain community:

> A class meeting does not have to be a big production. This class meeting might happen in line as we walk to lunch or the gym; it might happen on the bus on the way to a field trip or during a class transition from one activity to the next. If I have done this well, the kids don't even know that we've had a "meeting." This should feel like we're just talking. Because we are.
>
> (pp. 82–83)

We can talk to students about their goals and aspirations, specifi-cally asking with an open mind how schools either support or hinder their pathway toward freedom. *What aspects of school pro-mote connections? What improvements are needed to help students feel more connected within school? What can teachers or administrators do to ensure that students have a positive learning experience?* For primary students, I may inquire what teachers can do to make an envi-ronment feel more comfortable and welcoming or spend time unpacking what a sense of belonging means (or a welcoming

environment) before delving into those questions in indepen-
dent conferences with students.

Time and space for feedback are also important factors for
consideration. The place where conversations are held and
when one initiates a dialogue matters. As mentioned in
Chapter 5, we must understand how we show up in discussions where emotions and experiences are processed. If mirror
work and intentional practices to build trust are not prioritized, students will likely not reveal the truths that are needed
to inform change.

If I don't feel psychologically safe with someone or do not
believe that they have my best interest at heart, then I'm not
going to subject myself to a deep
conversation that is going to deplete
energy or ruin my vibe. We cannot expect students to shed light
on their experiences if we have not
cultivated an environment of trust
where belonging and accountability
to a community are felt.

> Mirror work forces us to recognize that we have much to learn as humans and some of us may need to shed the "know-it-all" complex that leads to defensiveness and hinders relationships.

The location of conferences should also be strategized. Some
students may not want to share certain thoughts in close proximity with others or may have a desire to share reflections outside of the classroom, perhaps with another adult who they
considered their "go-to" person. I have held student conferences over lunch, recess, or unstructured times within the
instructional day, and before or after school hours. It's not a
new practice to get to know students and understand their
needs to serve them best, but it is challenging to shift from
listening to action depending on the sociopolitical context of
schooling. When I worked as a chief equity officer in Hamilton
Southeastern Schools in Fishers, Indiana (one of the predominately white institutions I have referenced in this book), school
board members debated their way to national news over add-
ing gender identity to a non-discrimination policy. Similarly,
it is hard to convey to Black students that their lives matter,
if a school corporation bans conversations or attire promoting
racial equity or is sanctioned by the state to abandon discussions

about our country's scrofulous history with racism. If leaders within school districts are not actively working to eliminate the identity threats that students face (i.e., antisemitism, ableism, sexism, Islamophobia, etc.), it makes the work of an equity-minded educator difficult when striving to build a classroom culture that is in constant tension with school culture. *And how are the children?*

Listening Tours

For teachers and school administrators, it's necessary to gain a pulse of how students are operating in schools, recognizing that each student holds value and opinions that can inform cultural shifts within classrooms and systems. Listening to students means that we process what is relevant in their world and respond to what they care about. **Human work.** We learn what students need to express their cultural identities in authentic ways and determine the structures we need to put in place for an affirming space. As an administrator, I developed many listening tours that involved a space for different groups of students (e.g., racial, gender-sexuality alliances, religious diversity organizations, athletic teams, virtual learning focus groups, etc.) to convey their school lived experiences. Teachers and, in some cases, city level officials (i.e., mayor, community agencies) were invited to caregiver-based focus groups with the intent to form partnerships and inclusive communities.

When framing listening tours, I inform students or caregivers that my purpose is to gain insights to improve school systems and generate positive learning outcomes. It is a time for listening where protocols are offered to guide the conversations, and students or caregivers speak freely about their encounters and interactions within school environments. My voice is not centered in those spaces. The Four Agreements (e.g., *speak your truth*, *experience discomfort*, *stay engaged*, and *expect and accept non-closure*) from the book, *Courageous Conversations About Race* (Linton & Singleton, 2006) are helpful tools for framing conversations, yet I also emphasize the protocol that *"learning leaves, stories stay"* to stress that someone's narrative should not be shared without their permission outside of the listening space. Students can also create their own protocols for having a vulnerable conversation. Ask what they need to talk without limitations.

Although I think it's important for administrators and district-level leadership to hear from students to make informed decisions, teachers have the power to develop spaces for active listening in the classroom environment and beyond. The learning I have gained from listening tours has been invaluable. School improvement measures as well as teaching practices need to incorporate student voice and the unique perspectives of youth. The following student reflections have been documented (2016–2021) through listening tours while working with middle school and high school students:

- ◆ "Everyone is different, no one is the same. I dislike when people make generalizations."
- ◆ "I wish teachers would respect my pronouns and understand that my parents are not the best people to contact about my struggles with my gender identity. Sometimes, a student's home life isn't accepting, and school is the only place where we feel accepted … When a teacher or student makes our identity feel inferior or invalid, it can be devastating."
- ◆ "Not addressing school problems is the same as supporting it (e.g., racism, homophobia, etc.)."
- ◆ "My counselor refused to place me in honors courses in middle school due to my label as an ENL student. I'm in honors classes in high school now and doing okay but will always wonder if I could have excelled more if that counselor just believed in me and gave me a chance."
- ◆ "You know, we (students) do have a life outside of school. Some of us deal with really hard stuff that is bigger than a math quiz."
- ◆ "We are a lot more knowledgeable about political issues than they (teachers) think; we don't need to be so babied about things. Often, you'll find that having an open discussion leads to great conversation."
- ◆ "The school claims to value mental health but we don't ever acknowledge bipolar and schizophrenia disorders."

- ◆ "I feel like not a lot of teachers care about students anymore. It's just a lot of lecturing and then they're done."
- ◆ "We need to stop ignoring the hate and slurs of different groups of people. The only time it's ever been addressed is when it hits the news and has the possibility of injuring our 'precious' school image."
- ◆ "I wish we had an environment where we could talk about real issues that impact peers or friends without being seen as a snitch."

When we receive insights from students, we are called to act (Buchanan-Rivera, 2019). It is damaging for students' thoughts and requests to fall on inaction after inviting them to speak their truth. These are not sympathy tours where we take out our violins and start playing music as students cry out for change, but spaces that determine the progression of systems work for collective action. As an administrator, listening tours helped me to design intentional professional development, analyze the ways mental health is supported, and form better partnerships with families. Listening spaces have also prompted more learning opportunities to help teachers understand how to engage in civic discourse with students. No matter the format, listen to understand. Then, respond to what you heard by co-constructing cultural and curricular shifts with students.

Advocacy Spaces

There is a plethora of research that conveys how extracurricular activities build a sense of belonging and contribute to identity development (Blomfield & Barber, 2009; Christison, 2013). They also help students understand the power of community as everyone works as a collective for a particular cause. Student advocacy spaces focus on educational and social emotional needs, including proactive measures toward an equitable, inclusive school community. Students recognize their educational and human rights, using their voices as well as other forms of expression to identify what needs to be changed as allies and co-conspirators.

As an administrator, I developed a Student Alliance for Equity (SAFE) organization with Renee Isom, a teacher librarian in Fishers High School. We formed a summer retreat for students to think about their purpose and passion for addressing social justice issues. The students breathed life into their vision of eliminating stereotypes through events, specifically during lunch hours, that engaged peers in critical conversations about humanity. Giving students the opportunity to connect and collaborate through advocacy groups is a rewarding experience that fosters leadership skills. However, we must also remember that students should not be placed in a position to do the heavy lifting of manufacturing inclusive environments. Although I believe that students are capable of leading the way, I also hold the belief that they *should not have to* lead. I don't hold students responsible for adult-created problems and recognize that youth within advocacy spaces need to see educators (and adults in their lives) also mirror and model their drive as well as passion for change. Former students and brothers, Mustafaa and Tahaa Munir, describe why spaces like SAFE and other student advocacy groups are necessary in education:

> The power behind student advocacy groups in high schools and universities boils down to two things—freedom and focus. In my experience, these groups tend to have more freedom in exploring change because students aren't afraid to speak up, don't have to fit an often-rigid mold found in groups such as official student governments, and have passionate, creative minds behind it all. The success of such groups usually comes from their strict focuses. Student advocacy groups can be centered around a common religion, race, culture, sexual orientation, gender identity, etc. or simply, a goal. And that commonality becomes actionable capability with the right resources. A personal value I see in these groups is how they act as a learning opportunity. The school environment is not only a place to learn academically, but civically as well. By growing up, noticing faults in your community, working with similarly minded individuals, and advocating

for the betterment of your community, civic citizenry is promoted and practiced. These steps are much easier on the smaller, student scale and allow our future generations to exercise their civic rights and responsibilities to hopefully better the world for us all.

(Mustafaa)

Within student advocacy groups every event, every seminar, and every conversation are initiated with the purpose to educate. Education can be divided into two sectors: awareness and action. Awareness deals with informing those who do not know about the true state or inequalities of our world. Student advocacy groups can provide education about the system of institutional racism and help people understand the experiences of minoritized groups, including their cultures and faiths. Action revolves around educating them [people] on how they can improve, either by personal reflection and actions or through organizing events, petitions, or mobilizing people to come together to push for cause. Education is the most powerful tool we must continue to use in student advocacy groups to create a better future.

(Tahaa)

Affinity Spaces

Sometimes students (adults too) need healing spaces where they can exchange stories, center joy, and feel validated for their experiences. Affinity groups are places of empowerment and help to reduce a sense of marginalization when people, particularly those at the margins, are surrounded by others who share an aspect of their identity and make them feel visible. For historically marginalized groups that have experienced discrimination, it can be a wellspring for restoration where members discuss strategies for combating inequities and learn how to organize (Denevi & Richards, 2018; Bell, 2015). Critics who claim that affinity spaces are a form of exclusion (i.e., *"Why isn't there a white student union?"*)

are likely benefiting from inequitable systems that extend macro-affirmations where their identities are centered, welcomed, and normalized in society (Wickham-Hurst, 2019). Some people, including communities of color, may refuse to see the presence of whiteness in institutions and their own lives when disapproving of racial affinity groups and in those cases, I continue to do what is best for students and communicate the benefits as conveyed through research and personal experiences. Ignorance, bigotry, and hate cannot derail the work of affirming kids, and so I stress to teachers, **leadership matters**. Students need a place to grapple with their identities and affinity space can be a beautiful space for human development. Note: Within my experience, I have seen affinity spaces established in both elementary and secondary settings (mostly secondary).

Within the same high school and corporation where I developed SAFE, an organization called Future Black Leaders (FBL) was an established affinity group for Black students. This organization was formed by students who wanted to create a safe space for racially and ethnically diverse youth to exist authentically, elevate equity, and promote Black excellence. In predominantly white communities, research demonstrates that it is difficult for students of color to exist in environments where colorblind methodologies and racial biases thrive (Chapman, 2014). Racial battle fatigue (Smith, Hung, & Franklin, 2011) physically and emotionally harms communities of color when they are constantly positioned to defend their humanity, rights, and existence (for real, it's exhausting), and affinity spaces can serve as a refuge for students experiencing marginalization.

FBL devised a Black Student Leadership Summit to create an opportunity for youth in central Indiana to focus on the development and sustenance of racial affinity spaces that validate the experience of descendants from the African diaspora. Nearly 200 students from surrounding school districts participated in the first annual summit on March 12, 2019 and the participation almost doubled the following year before widespread news of the COVID-19 global pandemic. The summit incorporated guest speakers, including Black students from Marian University who talked about self-care and the value of community. Students were charged to create a vision board and goals for their organization with the support of adult sponsors and school administrators. Marc Williams, former FBL sponsor and current assistant principal conveyed:

> This [Black Leadership Summit] was intentional and gave students an opportunity to exercise a range of critical social and leadership skills. My role was mostly advisory, but I did spend some time during the summit giving some guidance to students from the perspective of an educator and a Black man. These types of events are fruitful as they intentionally focus on a group that is frequently overlooked in school and in society. I saw students take pride in their plans of action and build community across high schools.
>
> (Williams, personal interview, 2020)

Affinity spaces not only provide opportunities for connection and healing but can be a source of advocacy and empowerment. Science teacher and member of the AISalam foundation, Wafa' Safi describes how the Muslim Student Association at Hamilton Southeastern High School is a supportive space for Muslim youth she serves as a club sponsor:

> Members of the Muslim Student Association (MSA) come from diverse backgrounds, but they share one thing in common: their faith. Many of the kids are also first-generation Americans so they had that in common too. MSA is space where students can be true to themselves with peers who can pronounce their names properly. This [pronunciation of name] may not be a big deal to some, but this means everything to a student with a "not American" name. When things happen in the world, such as the Muslim ban during the Trump administration or the New Zealand shooting, the students can commiserate and grieve together. They can talk about their very real fears while surviving in a world that is often demoralizing to them. The love that students pour into each other

is incredibly healing. They feel understood and appreciated. MSA gives students the courage to stand tall and be proud of who they are through the development of various interfaith events (e.g., service projects, sponsored World Hijab Day, Friendship Day, Henna Days, etc.) and spaces where they can tell their story.

(Safi, personal interview, 2021)

Critical Conversations About Race in the Classroom

Through student conferences, listening tours and organizations we gain meaningful perspectives from students, yet we also need to focus on the work of driving critical dialogue in the classroom. It is important for students to have a strong sense of self through identity work, so they understand their relationship to others and sociopolitical contexts. Contrary to the cases state legislators are making to ban CRT in American schools (e.g., Texas, Arkansas, Tennessee, etc.), youth need to know truth and understand how the United States was built on a foundation of racial inequities and systems designed to marginalize people of color (Buchanan-Rivera, 2020)—*and I don't know of many K-12 teachers who are teaching CRT with fidelity as myself and others have on a collegiate level, so there's that.* Life and liberty for all was never intended for all and therefore we see such vivid brokenness, violence, and harm in our world as well as the fight to redistribute power. Following the murder of George Floyd and national protests, I was sickened by the number of viral videos of white youth who re-enacted the violence of Derek Chauvin and placed their knees on the necks of peers for a social media challenge. I wrote a blog post titled "A Plea to White Parents: Get Real About Race" (2020) due to the number of white allies who reached out to me personally in need of tools for starting critical conversations about race. The writing piece also acknowledged the complexities of identity, social construction, and how the strategies provided could benefit all racial identities as many people of color have been socialized in systems of whiteness. Before initiating conversations in the classroom, it is no surprise to hear me say that adults must do their own work first, which has been the intent of the mirror work throughout this book. Here is a recap of points made from that blog to help students with conversations about race:

- ◆ *Be transparent.* Discuss the beauty and strengths of cultural and racial diversity while being clear that we operate in systems that have historically marginalized Black and Brown communities. Most laws in history serve as receipts.
- ◆ *Engage students in identity work* (see Chapter 3), helping them to understand who they are and their relations to others.
- ◆ *Do not romanticize history.* Be honest with students as they deserve truth. "If you sang *Colors of the Wind*, while completely avoiding the talk about the misrepresentation of Disney's Pocahontas and the harmful effects of colonization, you experienced whiteness at work" (Buchanan-Rivera, 2020, n.p.). Talk to students about present injustices that stem from government sanctioned laws of the past and how many activists such as Jasilyn Charger, from the Cheyenne River Sioux Nation, are still fighting and advocating for human rights today.
- ◆ *Highlight achievements.* Discuss the achievements and contributions of people of color in the past and present (i.e., *James Baldwin, Dolores Huerta, Nikole Hannah-Jones, Zaila Avant-garde, etc.*). Talk about the resilience and strength of people of color who have been at the forefront of liberatory movements. Ensure you have texts and literature for an inclusive library that honors the voices of people of color.
- ◆ *Be an upstander.* Help students to understand the power of their voice and the harm that comes from silence. Teach students about the use of inclusive language and how to positively affirm members of a community (see Chapter 3).
- ◆ *Create an action plan.* Help students to create their own action plan to address racial inequities. How can they be a part of the change and what can be done in their spheres of influence? Give students opportunities to process and reflect on their own racial equity journey.

Critical conversations with youth can be the beginning of understanding allyship and co-conspiratorship, helping students to be a part of the journey of building a just society. Once students understand biases and how ideologies are shaped (see Chapter 3) they can become more mindful of their interactions and how they process social situations. Self-introspection helps students to think about the voices and beliefs that are centered as well as their impact from intentions. We all have choices. When faced with identity threats that are challenging and harmful to school culture:

>...we can choose to be apathetic and refrain from demonstrating care toward others.

>...we can choose to be complicit and remain silent despite how we feel inside.

>...we can choose to be responsive to someone's specific need after harm has occurred yet refrain from collective work to disrupt harmful systems.

>...we can choose to be a disruptor and interrupt harm, saying what needs to be said in the moment.

>...we can choose to be a mobilizer and organize people to be a part of a movement toward change that is bigger than ourselves.

We all have choices.

 **Mirror Work**

Think about how you enter critical conversations. *When you see something, do you say something? Is your voice louder on social media than real life? Where do you stand (e.g., apathetic, complicit, responsive, disruptor, or mobilizer) and does it depend on the circumstance?* For example, I am a community organizer and co-founder of a coalition called the Racial Equity Community Network (RECN). With a team of advocates, I am constantly mobilizing communities to combat racism at every level, but I know there have been moments in my life when I have been complicit and remained silent, especially when knowing the consequences of my truth-telling and the harm my family has experienced. I acknowledge that I am an imperfect person who carefully considers *when to push and when protect my peace*. This work comes with risks and we all have choices. Reflect on how you show up.

Brave Spaces

As discussed in Chapter 3, conversation stems and protocols can help to generate a strong level of engagement, but students still need support in navigating challenging conversations that pertain to complexities of humanity. There are times when insight and feedback are needed, and moments when we need to be reflective and consume information around us—*a balance that requires ongoing learning*. As a collective, teachers and students can develop agreements or norms that center the fostering of brave spaces and teach youth how to be mindful of the emotions, biases, and ideologies carried into learning experiences. Students need to practice civic discourse and should feel encouraged to speak truth. However, we must also be clear that speaking truth does not give anyone the permission to dehumanize someone else or place one's humanity on trial. When educators create conditions for empowerment, youth can authentically express and interrogate their understandings of the world and bring their whole selves into the classroom environment.

In my work of supporting educators, I have come across many teachers who lead with love and care for their students' humanity. There are classrooms that have a magical aura where you can feel the bonds of community and witness a spirit of collaboration. Students are not afraid to name what is a threat to justice. These environments do not happen accidently and it's beautiful to be an observer of such spaces. Ethics and US History teacher, Matt Bockenfeld, was one of those educators who consistently centered humanity in his work with students (including my collegiate level students when serving as an adjunct professor) and openly discussed his positionality as well as his commitment to advance racial equity as a white male—*something I do not see as often as needed in education*. His work was featured on *The Takeaway* podcast (2021) as a guest speaker alongside Gloria Ladson-Billings to discuss how educators tackle conversations about systemic racism. Bockenfeld (personal interview, 2021) shared the following on how he creates an environment for critical conversations:

+ *Do the pre-work.* No student will engage in hard conversations when their humanity hasn't been affirmed in your class. Prioritize students as humans first. That might even mean that some days, your planned lesson needs to be the lowest priority.
+ *Shatter your echo chamber.* Your echo chamber is dangerous, no matter who it consists of, because it reduces those not in it to outsiders. No student can ever be viewed as an outsider in your class. Students will disengage if they don't feel seen.
+ *Embrace vulnerability* by giving up control. It's not your classroom, it's our classroom. Consider what it would look like to give students real power to shape the culture of the room. The best classrooms don't help students find the right answers—they help them ask the right questions.
+ *Don't say—just do.* If you need to say things like, "In this class, we uphold the dignity of all students," you're using your position of power to try to enforce a code of conduct. But if you simply embody the core values of safe spaces, you're establishing a culture of dignity that draws students in.
+ *Listen* before you speak. Read before you write. Learn before you teach. Humility is our avenue to a more human classroom. When these pre-conditions are set, students absorb the unspoken truth that their voice matters.
+ *Meet students with grace* when they make errors. Conversations about race and humanity may be intimidating. When you show students that we are here to grow and not to judge, they will engage with enthusiasm.

LaMar Timmons-Long, a Black, New York City-based English educator, believes the classroom should be a brave space where students take risks, share authentic voices and perspectives, and evolve as human beings. He intentionally asks students what they need within a classroom environment to be brave and speak freely. Based on that question and dialogue from students, classroom norms are devised to create an empowering space. I interviewed LaMar Timmons-Long to learn more about the norms he develops with youth in the classroom. The following outlines some of the student-created norms in his classroom that derived from critical conversations:

1. *Trust*: Students want a space that embraces vulnerability where they can experience trusting relationships and respect each other.
2. *Active Listening*: Listening attentively to the person speaking with ears, head, heart, and body language. Also, making space for many voices to heard.
3. *Be open to the process*: Students want peers to be open to listening and receiving feedback, including praise or critiques.
4. *Varied perspectives*: We all have our own lived experiences; everyone's experience should be heard, valued, and respected.
5. *Agree/disagree, respectfully*: Students were aware that they would not always agree on every topic, idea, and position, and that's ok. However, we [as a collective] should be able to have a respectful dialogue about our differences for understanding.

Timmons-Long shares the following about his experience while co-constructing classroom norms with students:

When we created those norms, I was blown away, not because they are not capable of creating class norms, but because the students are always willing and ready for anything: to do "the work," share their voices, dialogue, and process together if the space is created for them. Lastly, I make it my mission to live by the notion "this is our space, so whatever we need to change and/or shift that will better the collective, then, let's do it." Why? Because they deserve to have autonomy over a space that is created for their voices, experiences and evolution. In our classroom, students have the ability to be critical and critical decision makers about text topics, text selection, and anything else needed to make our classroom a brave space to amplify their voices. In the end, we all benefit and evolve from the experience.

(Timmons-Long, personal interview, 2021)

Critical conversations are apt to happen in conditions that affirm identities where content is humanized. Identity affirming classrooms reflect teachers who see students as humans with an insatiable desire for learning. The classroom is an environment where perspectives can be embraced and broadened, and knowledge can be demonstrated through multiple means. Student engagement also increases when learners feel a part of a community. This is human work and our commitment to youth.

Chapter Highlights

- ◆ Equity actuates when we create spaces for listening and learning. Language is a powerful tool for justice-centered work and students need time to express thoughts about their school experiences.
- ◆ We can structure opportunities for listening in the form of personalized conferences, listening tours, or the development of student affinity or advocacy groups.
- ◆ Students are never too young to talk about justice and have critical conversations about race. If students can experience racism at a young age, then they can certainly talk about it in an environment that exhibits a culture of CARE with a teacher who's committed to mirror work and ABAR.

 **Collective Work**

When the core beliefs of schools indicate that environments are student-centered, think about what that means and how youth feel about their educational experiences? How are students, their passions, and full humanity centered? Within a professional group dynamic (e.g., grade level team, school improvement committee, equity-related team, professional learning community, etc.), review the following questions:

1. Name spaces or times within the classroom or school environment that are devoted to listening and honoring the perspectives as well as experiences of students.
2. Are there varied ways for students to demonstrate and express their comprehension of learning experiences?
3. What affinity spaces or advocacy groups exist in the school environment?
4. Do students feel like they are contributing members towards school-based decisions that support educational outcomes? If so, talk about the measuring stick. How do you know if students believe their contributions, opinions, and feedback matter?

References

Bell, M. (2015). Making space: Affinity groups offer a platform for voices often relegated to the margins. *Learning for Justice.* www.tolerance. org/magazine/summer-2015/making-space

Buchanan-Rivera, E. (2019, October 24). Identity-affirming classrooms need race-conscious teachers. *ASCD.* www.ascd.org/ascd-express/ vol15/num04/identity-affirming-schools-need-race-conscious- educators.aspx

Buchanan-Rivera, E. (2020, June 11). A plea to white parents: Get real about race. *Identity Affirming Space.* https://drbuchananrivera.com/ index.php/2020/06/11/a-plea-to-white-parents-get-real-about-race/

Blomfield, C.J., & Barber, B.L. (2009). Brief report: Performing on the stage, the field or both? Australian adolescent extracurricular activity participation and self-concept. *Journal of Adolescents*, *32*(3), 733–739.

Chapman, Thandeka K. (2014). Is integration a dream deferred? Students of color in majority white suburban schools. *The Journal of Negro Education*, *83*(3), 311–326. doi:10.7709/jnegroeducation.83.3.0311

Christison, C. (2013). The benefits of participating in extracurricular activities. *BU Journal of Graduate Studies in Education*, *5*(2), 17–20. https://files.eric.ed.gov/fulltext/EJ1230758.pdf

Denevi, E., & Richards, M. (2018). Frequently asked questions about affinity groups in k-12 schools. *Diversity and Equity Best Practices*. www.pps.net/cms/lib/OR01913224/Centricity/Domain/4870/2018%20Denevi%20Richards%20Affinity%20Groups%20FAQ.pdf

Linton, C., & Singleton, G. (2006). *Courageous Conversations About Race*. Thousand Oaks, CA: Corwin Press.

McMullen-Laird, L., & Yacob, P. (executive producers). (2008–present). The takeaway [Audio podcast]. *GBH, PRX & WNYC Studios*. www.wnycstudios.org/podcasts/takeaway/segments/how-educators-are-talking-students-about-systemic-racism

Minor, C. (2019). *We Got This*. Portsmouth, NH: Heinemann.

Smith, W., Hung, M., & Franklin, J. (2011). Racial battle fatigue and the miseducation of black men: Racial microaggressions, societal problems, and environmental stress. *The Journal of Negro Education*, *80*(1), 63–82. www.jstor.org/stable/41341106

Wickham-Hurst, K. (2019, June 1). Macro affirmations. *Mocha Momma*. www.kellywickham.com/mochamomma

Epilogue
A Love Letter to Those Doing the Work

In this fight for liberation, there are many oppositional forces that attempt to silence our voice and hinder our commitment to human work. Sometimes it is difficult to find our footing in this work of affirming identities when faced with challenges that strive to slow progression toward freedom. In the #31DaysIBPOC blog series designed by Kim Parker and Tricia Ebarvia (both co-founders of #DisruptTexts) to elevate writers of color, I wrote about my mantra when leading DEI work. There are times that require us to push, pause, and protect our peace.

- ◆ We need to push for truth-telling. My dear friend and educational scholar, Marian Dingle (in Strauss, 2021), reminds us that we have the choice to enable our students to think critically or make them resent us in years to come when they learn of withheld truths. We owe our students a rich perspective of history and its implications for the present. Talking about race in schools should not be a debate. Racism and racist ideologies are divisive. If we want to heal as a human race, we must acknowledge the truths about racism, power and privilege, and sociopolitical contexts that have shaped how humans navigate in a racialized society. Therefore, I am thrilled to see the phenomenal work of Sonja Cherry-Paul's edition of *Stamped* (Kendi & Reynolds, 2021) in the hands of children and respect the work of the #DisruptTexts movement led by Kim Parker, Tricia Ebarvia, Lorena Germán, and Julia Torres. As stated by Kelly Wickham-Hurst (2019), founder of Being Black at School, "racism is killing all of us, some more quickly than others."

DOI: 10.4324/9781003216964-10

♦ We need to push for equitable environments and question who benefits or is harmed by systems. The implementation of culturally responsive practices, newly learned and fresh out of a workshop, will be ineffective if in the hands of someone who lacks a critical consciousness and utilized in a system that is contradictory to responsive pedagogy (e.g., implementing highly effective reading strategies within an inequitable grading system that is failing students over missing assignments). Equity work is a verb that requires us to interrogate systems and remove barriers. Bettina Love (Love, Muhammad, & Simmons, 2020) reminds us that we cannot be in the business of managing inequities. The time is long overdue to dismantle them.

♦ We need to push for accountability as an act of love for the communities and people we serve. No longer are we in the position to wait for good intentions to come to fruition. Leadership matters. If a school is committed to affirming all students, all means all. An organization cannot represent a vision that values diversity while simultaneously upholding discriminatory practices. If you want to do real work, *say what you mean and mean what you say with your whole chest.* Do the work, holding yourself and others accountable.

♦ We need to push for listening spaces. At the heart of a community are humans who feel interconnected to each other's needs and understand that our liberation is bound together. As Fannie Lou Hamer (1971) challenged at the National Women's Political Caucus, "Nobody's free until everybody's free." Language is a tool of freedom and equitable environments cannot be created without the voices and perspectives of marginalized communities. Push for multiple perspectives, decenter yourself, hand over the mic when necessary, and amplify voices at the margins to have an understanding of different lived experiences with the purpose to effect change.

♦ We need to push for visibility of stories and identities that are continuously overlooked and erased within the curriculum. It's critical to analyze the voices that are commonly elevated in curricular content, decentering whiteness and providing opportunities for students to see themselves in learning experiences. We need to acknowledge institutional racism and how it is embedded in systems to perpetuate invisibility.

It's important to also think about the times we need to pause, recollect our thoughts, and regroup. We do not have all the answers in this fight for liberation. Jamila Lyiscott (2019) said that in social justice work, "we often become so consumed by what we are fighting against that we hardly take the time to truly envision the kinds of schools, communities, and societies that we are fighting for" (p. xiii). It's okay to take a step back and seek for others who can offer support, serving as accountability or thought partners. Betina Hsieh (2021), associate professor of teacher education at California State University, has helped me to deeply reflect on my journey towards justice. Two questions she has posed of many that have sparked deep, critical thinking are:

1. On whose shoulders do you stand?
2. For whom will you be an ancestor?

I stand on the shoulders of Cornelius Wilbourn (great-grandmother), Levater Greer (grandmother), Teresa Traylor (grandmother), and Jackie Greer-Buchanan (mother). All brilliant Black women who made sacrifices for me and wished greatness upon my life long before its existence. I carry them with me in this work and their collective experiences of navigating discrimination, Jim Crow laws, and misogynoir in society. It's important for me to pause and recenter myself, understanding my positioning and the legacy I want to leave behind when I exit this world.

Lastly, we all need to recognize when it's time to protect our peace, but I'll be clear that there are varying degrees to what this protection looks like for educators of color and white educators. For white educators, protecting peace does not mean avoiding discomfort, but rather reflecting on how you engage it. I need you to be uncomfortable, to call people out or in who look like you, and use your voice to specifically denounce racism among many other forms of oppression. For white educators, it may mean that you have to become strategic in your approach, press the pause button on a heated conversation and circle back to it, or step back to gain more clarity before pressing forward again. Yet, through it all you keep moving forward, taking a mental clarity break when needed and tagging yourself back in the disruptor role.

For educators of color, many of us need spaces for healing and restoration. Racism wears and tears on our bodies and minds in ways that are hazardous to health. Each day of writing this book, I have seen more pushback against CRT, SEL, and culturally responsive teaching in efforts to eliminate anything that could potentially lead to a conversation about race. It is exhausting to be in a constant state of defending your humanity. I have even found myself in confrontational spaces with people of color who have a proximity to whiteness, uphold racist ideologies, and echo rhetoric against CRT. Please choose self-love and know when you need to give your ears a rest for your wellness. As a person who battles racism in health care systems while advocating for my own life, the cortisol is not worth the manifestation of an illness. Continue to push for students and embrace co-conspirators who are empowered to fight the good fight. Know that you do not have to subject yourself to the harms of an institution that was not historically built for you to thrive and you don't have to do this work alone. If your "pushing" is causing you to lose sight of yourself, your health, and the ancestor you desire to be, protect your peace. This work is generational and it's not going away any time soon. I need you to take care of yourself.

Every day we are left with choices. Choose to love kids and their full humanity. Love yourself and commit to a process of healing and ongoing mirror work so you can see their full humanity. Give yourself grace while growing and learning. Hold your colleagues accountable out of love. Through love, we are compelled to create identity affirming environments and through a community of care we can make freedom dreams become a reality.

References

Hamer, Fannie Lou. (1971, July 10). *National Women's Political Caucus*. Washington, DC.

Hsieh, B. (2021, June 3). *We move Towards Equity When we Honor Humanity. [Virtual Workshop]*. Indianapolis, Indiana: Washington Township Schools.

Kendi, I., & Reynolds, J. (2021). *Stamped (for kids): Racism, Antiracism, and You. (Cherry-Paul, S.)*. New York, NY: Little Brown Books for Young Readers.

Love, B., Muhammad, G., & Simmons, D. (2020, June 23). *Abolitionist Teaching and the Future of Our Schools*. Haywood Books. www.haymarketbooks.org/blogs/179-abolitionist-teaching-and-the-future-of-our-schools

Lyiscott, J. (2019). *Black Appetite, White Food*. New York, NY: Routledge.

Strauss, Valerie. (2021, January 6). So educators, I ask you in all sincerity: What are you teaching tomorrow? *The Washington Post*. www.washingtonpost.com/education/2021/01/06/so-educators-i-ask-you-all-sincerity-what-are-you-teaching-tomorrow/

Wickham-Hurst, K. (2019, October 24). *Keynote Speaker. Racial Equity Community Network Kick-off*. Fishers, Indiana: Delaware Township Center.

Appendix A

Responsiveness Assessment for Classroom Environments (RACE)

Intentional spaces for belonging					
Self-evaluation ratings NA—Not Applicable NS—Not Sure	Rarely	Sometimes	Often	NA NS	**Reflective questions** Consider evidence when applicable.
Mirror work					
I intentionally think about the message(s) my classroom environment (e.g., layout, features, design, etc.) communicates to learners.	Rarely	Sometimes	Often	NA NS	*What are my beliefs about learners and their capabilities?*
I consider how I can co-construct learning environments with the voices and input of students.	Rarely	Sometimes	Often	NA NS	*What ideologies or beliefs do I carry with me while developing spaces of belonging?*
Systems work and conditions for learning					**Reflective questions** Consider evidence when applicable.
The policies and sociopolitical contexts of education influence how I arrange, design, and organize space in the classroom.	Rarely	Sometimes	Often	NA NS	*What does the environment invite students to learn or do based on its layout and design?*
There are spaces in the classroom that foster collaboration and connectivity.	Rarely	Sometimes	Often	NA NS	
Features within the classroom invite students to see themselves in learning experiences.	Rarely	Sometimes	Often	NA NS	*How does the environment foster identity development (students are able to learn more about themselves and who they are as learners)?*

(Continued)

Intentional spaces for belonging					
There is space for individualized work in the classroom.	Rarely	Sometimes	Often	NA NS	
There is space provided for small-group instruction.	Rarely	Sometimes	Often	NA NS	
Students have adequate space for mobility to engage in instructional activities.	Rarely	Sometimes	Often	NA NS	*How is learning represented within the classroom environment?*
Classroom materials are organized and accessible for student use.	Rarely	Sometimes	Often	NA NS	*How is student voice utilized in classroom design?*
The arrangement and design of space changes as I acquire more knowledge of the needs of a learning community.	Rarely	Sometimes	Often	NA NS	
Instructional materials are authentic and connect students to the natural world.	Rarely	Sometimes	Often	NA NS	
Authentic representations of learning					
Self-evaluation ratings	Rarely	Sometimes	Often	NA NS	**Reflective questions** Consider evidence when applicable.
Mirror work					
When I see something that is dehumanizing and harmful to humanity, I say something.	Rarely	Sometimes	Often	NA NS	*How do you stand up for justice? (e.g., within and outside of school contexts)*
I engage in critical conversations about race in school and social contexts outside of educational spaces.	Rarely	Sometimes	Often	NA NS	
Systems work and conditions for learning					**Reflective questions** Consider evidence when applicable.

(Continued)

Intentional spaces for belonging					
Students are given the opportunity to discuss their passions and topics they care about in the classroom environment.	Rarely	Sometimes	Often	NA NS	What spaces or times within the classroom or school environment are devoted to listening and honoring the perspectives as well as experiences of students?
Learning is represented in varied ways (e.g., writings, illustrations, debates, action research, etc.).	Rarely	Sometimes	Often	NA NS	
Students feel free to take risks, engage in discourse, and ask questions.	Rarely	Sometimes	Often	NA NS	
Students engage in critical conversations about humanity (e.g., race, justice, etc.).	Rarely	Sometimes	Often	NA NS	What affinity spaces or advocacy groups exist at school? Do students feel like they are contributing members toward school-based decisions that support educational outcomes? If so, talk about the measuring stick. How do you know if students believe their contributions, opinions, and feedback matter?
There are intentional spaces for learning and listening to understand the perspectives of students.	Rarely	Sometimes	Often	NA NS	
Identity affirmations					
Self-evaluation ratings	Rarely	Sometimes	Often	NA NS	**Reflection questions** Consider evidence when applicable.
Mirror work					
I engage in ongoing mirror work to better understand my own identity, ideologies, and how I show up to students.	Rarely	Sometimes	Often	NA NS	How do you identify yourself? Who has influenced your aspirations of self?
I am aware of the identities of students when determining and devising instructional practices for implementation.	Rarely	Sometimes	Often	NA NS	How were you taught to value differences?
I intentionally think about race, power dynamics, and sociopolitical contexts while working with students and developing learning experiences.	Rarely	Sometimes	Often	NA NS	How have your social experiences in the world influenced the way you see people who do not share your identity?

(Continued)

Intentional spaces for belonging

Systems work and learning conditions					Reflective questions Consider evidence when applicable.
Students actively engage in identity work or learning experiences that promote self-awareness (for human development and in efforts to build community).	Rarely	Sometimes	Often	NA NS	*What aspects of my lesson or unit of study promote self-love and reflect a mirror that affirms the identities of learners?*
Literature connects to the identities and histories of students, portraying positive images of their humanity.	Rarely	Sometimes	Often	NA NS	*How am I providing space for students to express their individuality and authenticity?*
Instructional materials and features within the classroom reflect the interests, histories, and identities of learners (e.g., race, gender, language, etc.).	Rarely	Sometimes	Often	NA NS	*How am I helping students to see their strengths and intellectual capabilities, and build self-confidence through the implementation of instruction?*
Students are given an opportunity to learn from their mistakes and are guided to think about the ideologies behind their actions for personal growth.	Rarely	Sometimes	Often	NA NS	*How am I creating a brave space for students to use their voice and understand its power?*

Humanizing approaches and the power of community

Self-evaluation rating Mirror work	Rarely	Sometimes	Often	NA NS	Reflective questions Consider evidence when applicable.
I embrace feedback and accountability in efforts to become a better human.	Rarely	Sometimes	Often	NA NS	*How do you see yourself or process your own emotions? Are you in touch with how you feel? How are you feeling at this moment?*
I recognize that good intentions alone do not yield equitable, just outcomes and purposefully think about my impact while serving students and their families.	Rarely	Sometimes	Often	NA NS	

(Continued)

Intentional spaces for belonging					
I think about the human condition and the emotions I carry into experiences while working with students, centering humanity in my pedagogy.	Rarely	Sometimes	Often	NA NS	How do the spaces you operate in (e.g., workplace, social circles, etc.) consider your humanity?

Systems work and conditions for learning					Reflective questions Consider evidence when applicable.
Students understand the concept of equity and are responsive to each other's needs, building a cohesive learning community.	Rarely	Sometimes	Often	NA NS	How can you foster caring relationships and partnerships within the classroom environment to create a sense of belonging?
The classroom is a brave space where students can process their emotions and experiences.	Rarely	Sometimes	Often	NA NS	Does the classroom environment honor the human condition?
Students see themselves as a part of a collective, taking responsibility for their actions and repairing harm when mistakes are made.	Rarely	Sometimes	Often	NA NS	
Students are provided time to connect and learn from each other, in efforts to build a sense of belonging.	Rarely	Sometimes	Often	NA NS	How does whiteness manifest in school spaces? How do you decenter whiteness and decolonize your classroom environment?
The curriculum honors the creativity and brilliance of students, eliciting authentic responses that do not stifle critical thinking or harm the humanity of learners (i.e., trauma, curriculum violence, etc.).	Rarely	Sometimes	Often	NA NS	

Support Material

Appendix A is also available as a free download so you can easily print a copy for your own use. Go to the book product page at routledge.com/9781032042930 and click on "Support Material" to access the download.

Appendix B
To Teachers who Face Resistance

In the Learning for Justice article, "Equity Work Should Start from the Top" (2019), we are reminded by Lauryn Mascareñaz and Rodney Trice that systemic cultural shifts necessitate support from leadership. From school boards to central office administration to principals and teachers, equity work must be prioritized and visible in actions as well as decision-making processes. However, from experience, I know there are leaders who are not equipped to address disparities due to either a lack of mirror work or ideologies that negate concepts of educational equity. Some leaders may also believe in doing the work but take detours to avoid conflict or community pushback. Here are my candid thoughts in ways to move forward when leaders may be the barrier:

1. *Amplify your voice.* Audre Lorde (1978) reminds us that "your silence will not protect you" nor will it protect the students you serve. If there's a need for change, take the time to collect your thoughts and articulate the why with evidence as well as possible action steps. Speaking truth may be uncomfortable, but as mentioned, the work of disrupting inequitable systems will come with risks. You may also discover in a courageous conversation with an administrator that they understand the concern(s) and have been engaged in behind-the-scenes work to improve conditions. I have worked with teachers who pointed fingers in my direction over what was not being done (during my principalship) while having no idea of the courageous discussions I held with district-level leadership and the wrist-slaps received for pushing or advocating for my teams. Work through the fear and assumptions by having a dialogue for understanding and clarification.

2. *Find your people.* Chapter 2 discussed the importance of finding your people. *Who are your mentors? People who can guide and challenge your thinking? Who are your north stars when reflecting on how you show up into the work?* Assemble a team of people and trusted colleagues who will publicly echo truths. Talk to your colleagues about the issues that should be raised in a group dynamic (e.g., *staff meeting, professional learning community, department chair meetings, etc.*). Have a meeting before the meeting. Collectively strategize your talking points to be clear in your delivery.

3. *Community organizing.* Still met with resistance and convicted in your beliefs that the lack of progress is harmful? Mobilize. Help families and community members to understand areas that require advocacy as well as who to contact. This is another move that comes with risks and great benefits if connecting with people who have the will to push while protecting you and the complicated relationship you have with the institution in the process. The Racial Equity Community Network (RECN) that I helped to co-found was born from several racial dialogues in the community where people discussed and learned about racial inequities in school systems. It ignited families to act, attend school board sessions, organize protests with students, and hold elected officials accountable to the vision of creating a vibrant city with a racial equity lens. When a community organizes, strategizes, and demands change, the movement can influence decision-making. Yet, remember that policies alone will not eradicate inequities. People must have the will to act.

4. *Choose you, choose freedom.* If you're in a place where you cannot find your people, lack community support, and are faced with the revelation that your beliefs of liberatory work run opposite of leadership views, you may need to find an environment that makes equity work visible. It is important to think about your mental health and physical well-being. When I contemplated leaving certain positions due to a misalignment between my beliefs and an institution's vision of equity, my heart immediately sank

thinking about the students and colleagues I would leave behind. However, I have learned that responsive teaching and equity-minded leadership will yield to lasting relationships that will follow one to any destination. Many of my former students are currently in college, starting careers, or taking care of their own families and still keep in touch to share meaningful milestones. You will not forget the connections you have made, nor will you or your work be forgotten or ceased. The seeds you planted along the way will grow and others will rise to move the work forward. Therefore, do yourself a favor, and take care of you in a supportive environment that knows your worth.

Do not be afraid to speak truth, find your people, lean into your community—*who can apply the pressure needed to disrupt systems*—and remember to save yourself, if needed.

References

Lorde, A. (1978). The transformation of silence into language and action. *Sinister Wisdom: A Journal of Words and Pictures for the Lesbian Imagination in All Women, 6*, 11–15.

Mascareñaz, L., & Trice, R. (2019, August 6). Equity work should start from the top. *Learning for Justice.* www.learningforjustice.org/magazine/equity-work-should-start-from-the-top